I0829258

SCHOOL

OF

CHEMICAL MANURES.

EXPERIMENTAL FIELDS OF VINCENNES.

See Page 50.

CULTURE OF WHEAT WITH CHEMICAL MANURES.

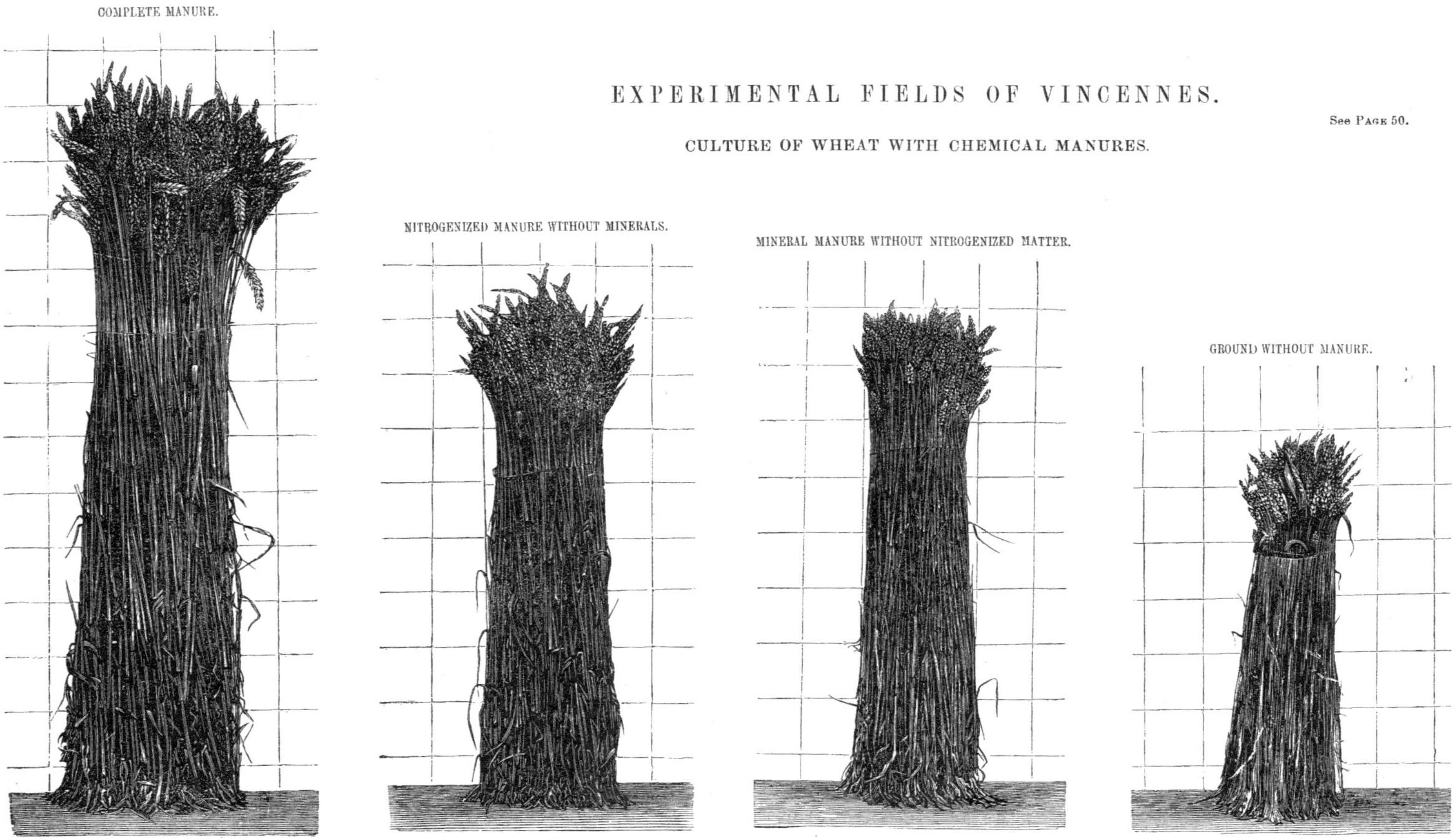

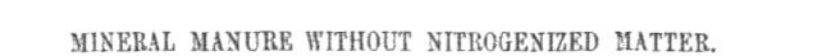

COMPLETE MANURE.

NITROGENIZED MANURE WITHOUT MINERALS.

MINERAL MANURE WITHOUT NITROGENIZED MATTER.

GROUND WITHOUT MANURE.

THE SCHOOL

OF

CHEMICAL MANURES;

OR

ELEMENTARY PRINCIPLES

IN THE

USE OF FERTILIZING AGENTS.

FROM THE FRENCH OF

M. GEORGE VILLE,

BY

A. A. FESQUET,
CHEMIST AND ENGINEER.

PHILADELPHIA:
HENRY CAREY BAIRD,
INDUSTRIAL PUBLISHER,
406 Walnut Street.
1872.

Collins, Printer, 705 Jayne St., Philada.

PREFACE.

After the long controversies of the opposite schools of nitrogenized manures *versus* mineral ones, and conversely, it is refreshing to find that they may be agreed upon the common platform—that every plant needs nitrogen as well as mineral substances for its food. This important result, as well as the rational manner of determining the natural fertility of the soil and the dominant substances for the food of plants, has been demonstrated by Professor Geo. Ville after thirty years of comparative experiments conducted in the field and in the laboratory, and checking each other. Moreover, at the present time, several hundred farmers in Europe and in the colonies follow the advice of the learned professor of vegetable physiology, and by their correspondence confirm the truth of his teachings.

Chemical manures do not mean strange and unknown substances, new to the farmer; they simply include phosphorus, lime, potassa, and nitrogen, that is to say, the useful substances found in any serviceable manure, compost, etc., from time immemorial. They are in a condensed form, nearly constant in composition, and may be readily mixed in various proportions to suit the nature of the desired crop, or the degree of the natural fertility of the soil. Moreover, with them, the farmer will be less exposed to frauds than when he buys manures already mixed, which, too often, are but nondescript compounds.

Manuring with chemicals alone has been proved by Prof. Ville and his followers to be profitable; nevertheless, other manures and compounds may be used in connection with them, but their usefulness as plant food will be in the ratio of the phosphorus, lime, potassa, and nitrogen which they contain in the *soluble or available state.*

When once the farmer has arrived at a knowledge of the natural fertility of his farm by the aid of experimental fields, as explained in this work, he will be able to compound his manures for each desired crop, without expending money for what is already in the soil, or omitting what is wanting. How much more desirable to do so, and to work with certainty, than to buy already mixed manures from the manufacturer, who, supposing that he is honest, can certainly know little, if anything, about the natural fertility of the soil, the previous manuring, or the rotation of crops on the farm of the purchaser.

This little book, written in a familiar dialogistic form, and intended for popular use, is a *résumé* of several larger works by the same author. We hope that it will be found interesting and useful, not only by farmers, but also by all those persons who have a fondness for agriculture.

A. A. F.

PHILADELPHIA, June, 1872.

NOTE.

The French metric decimal weights, measures, and values have been retained in this translation for the sake of clearness and facility in comparing together the various formulæ and results of experiments. Moreover, the money values given in this work, if translated into American currency, would not answer the American market prices of the various substances.

For those desirous of transforming into English the French weights, measures, and values mentioned in this work, we give the following tables:—

1 centimetre	= 0.3937 inch.
1 metre	= 3.2809 feet.
	= 1.0936 yard.
1 square metre	= 10.7643 square feet.
	= 1.196 square yard.
1 are	= 100 square metres.
	= 119.6033 square yards.
1 hectare	= 100 ares.
	= 2.4711 acres.

1 hectolitre	= 3.5316 cubic feet.
	= 2.8379 U. S. bushels of 2150.42 cubic inches.
1 kilogramme	= 2.2055 lbs. avoirdupois.
1 tonne (*ton*)	= 1000 kilogrammes.
	= 2205.486 lbs. avoirdupois.
1 franc	= about $0.19 (gold).

As a means of converting quantities and values as applied to the *hectare* into the corresponding quantities and values per *acre*, the following table will be found useful:—

PER HECTARE.	PER ACRE.
100 kilogrammes	= 89.291 lbs. avoirdupois.
1 tonne (*ton*)	= 892.91 " "
1 hectolitre	= 1.1489 U. S. bushel.
100 francs	= $7.69 (gold).

1 franc per kilogramme	= 8.61 cents (gold) per lb. avoirdupois.
1 franc per 100 kilogrammes	= 8.61 cents (gold) per 100 lbs. avoirdupois.
10 francs per 100 kilogrammes	= $0.861 (gold) per 100 lbs. avoirdupois.

CONTENTS.

CHAPTER I.

PAGE
FORMATION and composition of plants 13
Fertility and sterility of soils 14
Farm-yard manure and chemical manure . . . 17
Complete chemical manure 17

CHAPTER II.

The particular action of each of the substances of the complete manure 18
The suppression of one of these substances is sufficient to considerably diminish and even annihilate the power of the others 19

CHAPTER III.

Aptitude of certain plants for extracting from the air the necessary nitrogen, which, therefore, may be dispensed with in the chemical manure . . . 21
With these plants the mineral manure possesses as much efficacy as the complete manure . . . 21

CHAPTER IV.

Assimilability of manures in general . . . 25

CHAPTER V.

PAGE

Each of the four constituent parts of the complete manure has in its turn a preponderating or subordinated action 34

CHAPTER VI.

The bases for profit in agriculture 50
Manures are the raw materials of the crops . . 51
Yields obtained with an expense of 150 to 200 francs of chemical manure per hectare 53

APPENDIX.

Ploughing and preparing the soil 59
Methods of using chemical manures 62

FORMULÆ OF MANURES.

Wheat 67
Barley, oats, rye, natural pastures 67
Hemp, rape-seed (colza) 68
Beets, carrots, cabbages, hops, gardening . . 68
Potatoes 69
Grape-vines and small trees 70
Turnips, rutabagas, Jerusalem artichokes, sorgho, sugar-cane, maize 70
Beans, horse-beans, peas, clover, sainfoin, vetches, lucern 71

ROTATION OF CROPS.

FIRST CASE.

PAGE

The chemical manures are employed alone without admixture of stable manure 72
Exclusive culture of wheat 72
Alternate culture of rape-seed (colza) and wheat . 74
Rotation of four years, comprising: potatoes, wheat, clover, wheat 75
Rotation of four years, comprising: beets, wheat, clover, wheat 76
Rotation of five years, comprising: potatoes, wheat, clover, colza, wheat 77
Rotation of two years, comprising: maize, wheat . 78
Rotation of six years, comprising: flax, beets, wheat, colza, wheat, and oats, rye, or barley 79
Rotation with fodder plants 81
Manures for pasture (forages) 82

SECOND CASE.

The chemical manures employed as auxiliary to farm-yard manure 83
Rotation comprising: potatoes, wheat, clover, wheat, oats 84
Rotation comprising: beets, wheat, clover, wheat, oats 86
Rotation comprising: colza, beets, wheat, clover, wheat 87
Rotation of six years, comprising : flax, beets, wheat, colza, wheat, and oats, rye, or barley 89
Experimental fields 91
Experimental field for a primary school 92
Culture of wheat 92
Composition of the manure intended for the experimental fields of a primary school 95

PAGE
Experimental field for the analysis of the soil . . 97
Series for wheat 100
Series for beets 102

VOCABULARY OF CHEMICAL MANURES.

Nitrogenized substances 105
Sulphate of ammonia 106
Nitrate of soda 107
Nitrate of potassa 108
Phosphate of lime 109
Sulphate of lime 111

THE

SCHOOL OF CHEMICAL MANURES.

CHAPTER I.

Formation and composition of plants—Fertility or sterility of soils—Farm-yard manure and chemical manures—The complete chemical manure.

The Professor. The objects of agriculture are to produce and multiply the useful plants and animals. Therefore, agriculture is of the first importance in social economy, since we rely upon it for food, raiment, and those animals which aid us in our daily labors.

We shall examine in the following pages only that which relates to the formation of plants, and to the processes by which they are profitably grown.

2

During the first period of their existence, plants find in the seed the substances necessary to their growth. Afterwards they borrow from other sources, and from that time we shall follow their development.

QUESTION. From whence come the substances necessary to the formation of plants?

ANSWER. We have already said that, during germination, the primary food is entirely derived from the seed. Later, the air, water, and soil furnish the nourishment. Plants extract that nourishment from the air by their leaves, and from the soil by their roots.

Q. Can plants extract from the air all that is necessary for their growth?

A. Never; they must also take from the soil certain substances which are found there only.

Q. Is the soil always provided with those substances necessary for vegetation?

A. Far from it; they are often wanting. Whereas the composition of the air is constant everywhere, that of the earth is exceedingly variable, and therefore modifies its fertility and properties.

Q. Is it possible always to obtain fine crops from the same soil which is simply tilled, and mechanically prepared, according to practical routine?

A. No. Under such a regimen the crops rapidly diminish, and the soil grows poorer.

Q. Crops therefore exhaust the soil?

A. It is a fact demonstrated by universal experience.

Q. What is the difference between a soil naturally barren, and one exhausted by culture?

A. There is no difference. Both will produce bad crops, because they are equally wanting in those substances without which plants cannot thrive. A naturally barren soil has never possessed these substances, and the exhausted one has lost them in the crops grown upon it.

Q. What is then to be done to preserve the fertility of the soil?

A. Restore to it, under certain forms,

those elements which have been borrowed from it by successive crops, and without which, we repeat, there is no durable production.

Q. And for rendering fertile a soil which is naturally barren?

A. We must enrich it with the same substances which we restore to worn-out soils. To sum up, we must *manure.*

Q. How is soil generally manured?

A. By mixing with it the excretions and litter of animals, which are known under the name of farm-yard manure.

Q. How does such a manure act upon the soil?

A. It acts by its *nitrogenized matter*, *phosphate of lime*, *potassa*, and *lime*, which are the indispensable agents for keeping up the fertility of soils, and obtaining all kinds of crops.

Q. Does farm-yard manure contain but these four substances?

A. It contains at least ten more, which it is not necessary to consider, since plants always find them in the earth and in the air.

Q. Barren or exhausted soils are therefore wanting in nitrogenized matter, phosphate of lime, potassa, and lime?

A. Precisely so.

Q. With these four substances, is it always possible to render a soil fertile?

A. Yes, it is always possible to obtain fine crops.

Q. Is it necessary, for their efficacy, that these four substances should be in the shape of farm-yard manure?

A. It is not necessary. Their mixture in the form of chemical products possesses the same properties.

Practically, the chemical manure is more powerful than that of the farm-yard. This will be easily understood, since in the farm-yard manure the four substances are mixed with foreign matters which hinder their action. On the other hand, the chemical manure is composed only of substances which act directly, and the absorption of which by the plants is rapid and certain. Therefore, in order to remember the certainty of its action, we shall call it the *complete manure*.

There is the same difference between the complete manure exclusively formed of chemical products, and the farm-yard manure, as there is between a metal and its ore, or pure quinine and the bark from which it is extracted. The ore contains the metal mixed with earthy matters; and the cinchona bark holds quinine amid a quantity of worthless ligneous substances. The chemical manure is a manure without useless materials.

CHAPTER II.

The particular action of each of the substances of the complete manure—The suppression of one of these substances is sufficient to considerably diminish, and even annihilate, that of the three others.

QUESTION. In order to obtain fine crops, is it absolutely necessary that the soil should contain nitrogenized matter, phosphate of lime, potassa, and lime, that is to say, the four substances of the complete manure?

ANSWER. It is absolutely necessary.

Q. What will happen, should the soil be wanting in one of these four substances?

A. Notwithstanding the presence of the other three, the vegetation remains languid, and the crops are poor.

Q. How can we ascertain that it is so?

A. It is very easily proven. In the experimental fields of Vincennes, for instance, a soil of inferior quality was chosen, and cultivated for several years, without any manure, until the crops had dwindled to next to nothing. Then the ground was subdivided into six parcels each equal to an *are* (about 119 square yards), and contiguous to each other.

The first parcel received no manure whatever, and there was scarcely any crop.

Potassa was added to the second, without better results.

The third parcel received phosphate of lime, and the crops were equally poor.

The same results were observed with the fourth and fifth parcels, one of which had received lime, and the other nitrogenized matter.

The sixth was provided with the mixture of nitrogenized matter, phosphate of lime, potassa, and lime, that is, the complete manure, resulting in a splendid growth, and a crop superior in quality and quantity.

But that was not all: a seventh parcel of the same ground was manured with phosphate of lime, potassa, and lime, that is to say, the complete manure without nitrogenized substance, and the results were as poor as if only one of the three substances had been employed.

The superiority of the complete manure proves that its results are essentially due to the collective action of the four associated substances. And in terminating this chapter, we would say that by the *mineral manure* we mean the reunion of phosphate of lime, potassa, and lime, that is, the complete manure less the nitrogenized matter.

CHAPTER III.

Aptitude of certain plants for extracting from the air the necessary nitrogen which, therefore, may be dispensed with in the chemical manure—With these plants the mineral manure possesses as much efficacy as the complete manure.

QUESTION. If it be true that the complete manure is the only efficient one, because it contains all the substances required for the life of plants, does it not follow that the mineral manure, deprived of nitrogenized matter, will be of little value?

ANSWER. This is true, indeed, for the majority of vegetables; there are, however, certain plants which thrive as well with the mineral as with the complete manure.

Q. Which are these plants?

A. Peas, beans, lucern, clover (trefolium), sugar-cane, etc., are among the most important ones.

Q. These plants, then, do not contain nitrogen?

A. On the contrary, they hold a great deal of it. A crop of lucern, for instance, contains two or three times as much nitrogen as a wheat crop.

Q. Well, then, where does the nitrogen of these plants come from?

A. From the air, which consists of four-fifths nitrogen.

Q. Why is nitrogen made a part of manures, since the air holds so much of it?

A. Because most of the plants do not possess the property of extracting it from the air. In regard to this, plants may be divided into two groups: the first comprises those plants which draw their nitrogen from the air, and the second those which take it preferably from the soil. The organization of vegetables presents this contrast, and in the practice of manuring we are obliged to distinguish plants requiring the complete manure, from those the development of which is complete with the mineral manure.

Q. Will plants, requiring a nitrogenized manure, also draw nitrogen from the air?

A. Yes, but in smaller proportion, and provided that the soil be supplied with nitrogenized matter, which insures their first development.

Q. Is it known in what proportion the soil and air furnish nitrogen for the principal crops?

A. Here are the proportions indicated by carefully made experiments.

Nitrogen	From the air	From the soil.
Clover	The whole	none
Barley	80 p. c.	20 p. c.
Rye	80 "	20 "
Wheat	50 "	50 "
Beets	60 "	40 "
Rape or cole-seed (Colza)	70 "	30 "

Q. How can we prove that it is so, and that clover or peas, for instance, take no nitrogen from the earth, and draw it all from the air?

A. It may be proved in two different ways: by laboratory experiments, and by culture in the field. Let us speak first of the laboratory experiments, because the results are simple and certain.

A sample of earth was calcined in a porcelain furnace, in order to destroy all nitrogenized substance which may have existed in it; this earth was then mixed with phosphate of lime, potassa, and lime, and watered with pure distilled water. Clover, sown in it, grew perfectly well, and the crop being analyzed demonstrated the presence of a large proportion of nitrogen, evidently due to the air, since there was none in the soil.

The practical proofs are not less certain. When a soil is cultivated without manuring, the crops become poor very rapidly. When wheat is grown every other year, the crop is better; if wheat alternates with horse-beans, which contain a great deal of nitrogen, the yield of wheat does not diminish. Indeed, the rotation with horse-beans is nearly as favorable to wheat as a year of fallow land. Why is it so? Because horse-beans draw their nitrogen from the air, whereas wheat extracts it from the soil.

CHAPTER IV.

Assimilability of manures in general.

The Professor. Manures are said to be assimilable, or available, when the plants are able to absorb them; and plants will absorb them only when the substances are soluble. It is generally acknowledged that farm-yard manure will produce all its effect only when sufficient dampness in the soil causes its decomposition.

Question. It may then happen that substances holding nitrogen, phosphate of lime, potassa, and lime, in large proportions, will be without action upon vegetables?

Answer. We will demonstrate it by an example relating to nitrogenized matters. Agriculture has, for a long time, utilized the waste of horn and woollen rags; but it has been ascertained that large pieces of horn have scarcely any effect, because they are too slow of decomposition, and their nitrogen does not become soluble. Only finely divided horn is now employed, which is rapidly decomposed.

Another striking instance is leather, that is to say, skin rendered insoluble and durable by the tanning process. The nitrogen of the skin is available, while that in leather is not. Skin is a good manure, and leather is a poor one.

Q. Is it the same in regard to phosphate of lime, potassa, and lime?

A. The good effects of these three products are subordinated to their solution. There are a great many substances, holding phosphate of lime, potassa, and lime, and which however do not act as manures, because they are not assimilated by the plants. For instance, there are large natural deposits of phosphate of lime, which cannot be used, unless it has been rendered assimilable by treatment with sulphuric acid. The same observation may be applied to granite and porphyry, with which whole mountain ranges are formed, and which cannot be employed as manures, notwithstanding their large percentage of potassa and lime, since these substances are in an insoluble state, and, therefore, without action upon plants.

Q. We may then go so far as to conceive a soil rich in nitrogen, phosphate of lime, potassa, and lime, and still be sterile however?

A. There is a great deal of correctness in this supposition, because natural soils hold a great portion of their elements of fertility in the insoluble state, and without any more effect upon crops than sand, clay, and gravel.

Q. Shall we, however, consider as entirely useless these natural elements of fertility which are not assimilable?

A. No, because by the combined action of light, heat, air, dryness, frost, etc., these elements are slowly decomposed and become soluble, but not sufficiently so to produce good crops. This explains the usefulness of fallow lands. The elements of the soil which have become soluble, during the fallow year, are absorbed by the plants grown the year after.

Q. Which are the commercial products holding assimilable nitrogen, and which may be used in agriculture?

A. The sulphate of ammonia, nitrate of soda, nitrate of potassa, and substances of animal origin, such as poudrette, blood and flesh dried, horn, woollen rags, etc.

Q. What is the percentage of nitrogen in these various products?

A. Sulphate of ammonia holds about twenty per cent. of nitrogen, nitrate of soda fifteen, and nitrate of potassa fourteen. We shall not mention the animal substances, because they have been subject to so many frauds that their yield is exceedingly variable.

Q. Is it indifferent whether we employ the sulphate of ammonia, or the nitrates, as nitrogen compounds?

A. We may, as a rule, employ either; but agricultural practice teaches us to prefer the nitrates for beets and potatoes, and the sulphate of ammonia for rapeseed and the cerealia.

Q. May we indifferently employ nitrate of soda, or nitrate of potassa?

A. No, because soda is without action upon the plants, whereas potassa is very important. The nitrate of soda is useful as far as the nitrogen it contains, while the nitrate of potassa is also valuable on account of its potassa.

Q. With an equal amount of nitrogen, are animal substances as valuable as the sulphate of ammonia and the nitrate of soda?

A. No, because during their decomposition a certain proportion of their nitrogen escapes in the air in the form of nitrogen gas, with which the atmosphere is already abundantly provided.

Q. That portion of nitrogen from animal substances, which acts upon plants,—in what form is it absorbed?

A. In the form of a nitrate or of some ammoniacal salt.

Q. What is the proportion of lost nitrogen during the decomposition of animal substances?

A. About 30 per cent. of the whole of the nitrogen.

Q. What are the chemical products holding phosphate of lime?

A. Bone dust, bone black from sugar-houses; and the superphosphate, or acid phosphate, of lime.

Q. What is the percentage of phosphate of lime in bone dust?

A. About 60 per cent.

Q. Where does the bone black come from?

A. From sugar-refineries, which employ it for decolorizing raw sugar.

Q. What is its origin?

A. The bones of animals which have been calcined in closed vessels.

Q. How much phosphate of lime is there in bone black from sugar-houses?

A. Its yield varies between 45 and 60 per cent.

Q. What is the meaning of acid phosphate of lime (superphosphate)?

A. Any kind of phosphate which has

become soluble by treatment with sulphuric acid.

Q. What is the proportion of soluble phosphate in the commercial acid phosphates?

A. *About* 40 per cent.

Q. In what form does phosphate of lime produce the best effects?

A. In that of acid phosphate, which is also called superphosphate of lime.

Q. Which are the commercial products holding potassa, and which may enter into the composition of chemical manures?

A. The nitrate of potassa, also known under the names of nitre and saltpetre, and which is preferable to all others.

Q. Have you not already mentioned this product as one of the best nitrogen compounds?

A. Yes, because it contains 14 per cent. of nitrogen and 47 per cent. of potassa, either of which is assimilable, and their union increases their mutual efficacy.

Q. Are there no other potassa materials but saltpetre?

A. We have the potassa of wood-ashes, and the refined potassas of various origins.

Q. What are the characteristics of refined potassa?

A. It is a white substance, very soluble in water, attracting the dampness of the air, and absorbing it in large proportions.

Q. What is the yield of refined potassa?

A. About 52 per cent. of real potassa.

Q. Which is to be preferred, nitrate of potassa or refined potassa?

A. Nitrate of potassa is preferable, because its potassa costs 0.75 franc per kilogramme, whereas that of the refined potassa amounts to 1.50 franc per kilogramme.

Q. Is not the nitrogen of the nitrate of potassa sometimes objectionable?

A. Practically, never.

Q. Have you not already said that there are vegetables which thrive just as well upon the mineral as upon the complete manure?

A. It is true; but even with these

vegetables, it is preferable to employ nitrate of potassa instead of refined potassa, because its price is lower, and its proportion of nitrogen too small to be objectionable.

Q. Which are the substances containing lime in an assimilable state, and which may enter into the composition of the complete manure?

A. The sulphate and carbonate of lime, that is, plaster of Paris and chalk.

Q. Which of the two is preferable?

A. Plaster of Paris (sulphate of lime).

Q. How so?

A. Because it is more soluble.

Q. Are the good effects of commercial manures due to the four substances of the complete manure?

A. They are due to these substances.

Q. Why should we prefer chemical manures to them?

A. We have already given the reason. They are entirely soluble, and, consequently, more certainly and rapidly absorbed by the vegetables. To this advantage we shall add that, their composition being fixed and invariable, they cannot be falsified without risk of judicial proceedings, which is a guarantee for the farmer.

CHAPTER V.

Each of the four constituent parts of the complete manure has in its turn a preponderating or subordinated action.

QUESTION. Each of the constituent parts of the manure is equally important for every kind of plant, is it not?

ANSWER. Far from it: each constituent part has such a predominating action over the other three, in regard to certain plants, that it will regulate the production.

Q. Does this regulating and predominating action continue even in the absence of the other constituent parts of the manure?

A. Yes and no. Yes, if the soil be naturally provided with the substance which is wanting in the manure; and no, if the soil itself does not contain it.

Q. In other words, may we not say that the predominating action ceases when the other constituent parts of the manure are absent?

A. Precisely so.

Q. The degree of importance of each substance of the complete manure is therefore subordinated to the nature of the plants to which it is applied, is it not?

A. Yes, and in order to remember this remarkable effect, we shall call *Dominant* that of the four substances, the action of which predominates over the other three for a given plant.

Q. What are the plants upon which nitrogenized matter has a predominating action?

A. Wheat, and generally all the cerealia, such as barley, oats, rye, to which we add rapeseed (colza), beets, hemp, etc.

Q. What are the plants most influenced by potassa?

A. Peas, beans, horse-beans, clover, sainfoin, vetches, lucern, flax, potatoes, etc.

Q. What are the vegetables upon which the action of phosphate of lime is greatest?

A. Maize, Jerusalem artichokes, ruta-bagas, turnips, radishes, sugar-cane, etc.

Q. And lime?

A. It does not appear to possess a marked preponderating action upon plants, although it is necessary everywhere.

Q. What conclusion do you draw from these indications?

A. That, in practice, we should reduce to their minimum the proportions of the subordinated substances, and increase that of the dominant substance.

Q. Could you give more weight to these indications by some example of agricultural practice?

A. We are able to do so. We have been taught by experience that with the following manure:—

	Per hectare.
Acid phosphate of lime . . .	400 kilogrammes
Nitrate of potassa	200 "
Nitrate of soda	300 "
Sulphate of lime	400 "

in which the nitrogen, represented by the nitrates of potassa and soda, amounts to 73 kilogrammes, we were able to obtain 47,323 kilogrammes (47.323 tons) of beets per hectare.

If the proportions of phosphate of lime, potassa, and lime be increased, the yield remains the same, no more, no less. On the other hand, by raising the proportion of nitrogen from 73 to 100 kilogrammes, the crop is increased from 47.323 to 51 tons. Should the proportion of nitrogen be still greater, 130 kilogrammes for instance, we gather 59.660 tons of beets.

Q. But, in balancing accounts, is there any profit in so increasing the proportion of nitrogen?

A. The advantage is great.

Q. Could you prove it by means of figures?

A. With the manure holding 73 kilogrammes of nitrogen we obtain 47.323 tons of beets, and 59.660 tons with a proportion of 130 kilogrammes of nitrogen. Therefore, with an increase of about 60 kilogrammes of nitrogen, value 120 francs, we obtain an overplus of 12.337 tons of beets, the value of which is 247 francs.

Q. What you have said about beets is also true in regard to other plants, is it not?

A. It is perfectly true, and here is another proof; with the following manure:—

	Per hectare.
Acid phosphate of lime	400 kilo.
Nitrate of potassa (nitrogen 28 kilo.) .	200 "
Sulphate of lime	400 "

in which the nitrogen amounts to 28 kilogrammes, there has been obtained at the Guadeloupe 40 tons of sugar-cane (without the leaves).

By raising the proportion of phosphate of lime from 400 to 600 kilogrammes, the yield went up from 40 to 84.782 tons of sugar-cane. Therefore, with an additional quantity of 200 kilogrammes of phosphate of lime, price 32 francs, the overplus of the crop was such as to amount to 800 francs.

Q. The nitrogenous matter being the dominant substance in manures for cerealia, there should be great advantage in applying large doses of it?

A. The advantage is evident, provided, however, that we should remain within certain limits, otherwise it may cause real injury.

Q. How can large proportions of nitrogen be injurious?

A. By causing such a luxurious growth that, should the season be a rainy one, the cerealia will be lodged, and the result will be a great deal of straw and little grain.

Q. It becomes evident that it is highly important that the proportions of chemical manures should be accurately determined. Therefore, what should be the manure for wheat?

A. The complete manure No. 1, the composition of which is as follows:—

	Per hectare.
Acid phosphate of lime . .	400 kilogrammes.
Nitrate of potassa	200 "
Sulphate of ammonia . . .	250 "
Sulphate of lime	350 "

Q. Is this manure equally suitable for beets?

A. A good crop would certainly be obtained with it. However, it is preferable to replace the 250 kilogrammes of sulphate of ammonia by 300 kilogrammes of nitrate of soda, and we then have the complete manure No. 2:—

	Per hectare.
Acid phosphate of lime . . .	400 kilogrammes.
Nitrate of potassa	200 "
Nitrate of soda	300 "
Sulphate of lime	300 "

Q. And for potatoes?

A. We should suppress the nitrate of soda of the preceding manure, and increase one-half the proportion of nitrate of potassa. We then have:—

	Per hectare.
Acid phosphate of lime . . .	400 kilogrammes.
Nitrate of potassa	300 "
Sulphate of lime	300 "

Q. And for maize, which is such an important crop for the south of France?

A. We should employ more phosphate of lime than with the potato crop, and reduce the proportion of nitrate of potassa to 200 kilogrammes. Thus:—

	Per hectare.
Acid phosphate of lime . . .	600 kilogrammes.
Nitrate of potassa	200 "
Sulphate of lime	400 "

But, as it is difficult to set down figures during a conversation, we would suggest that all similar questions on manure should be referred to the appendix of this work, which contains a special chapter where we have gathered all the formulæ from our own experience, and where the chemical manures are considered either alone or in connection with stable manure.

Q. One word more. With the employment of chemical manures, what are the expenses and profits?

A. Taking as an average a rotation of crops of four years' duration, and composed of the following cultures:—

1st year, ...	potatoes.
2d "	wheat.
3d "	clover.
4th "	wheat.

The annual expense in manures varies from 180 to 200 francs per hectare, and the profit from 200 to 300 francs.

Q. Can these formulæ be applied to all kinds of soils indifferently?

A. It is possible, as a general rule. Indeed, we should not deviate from them at the beginning. But, later, when we have become conversant with the laws of the production of vegetables, it is preferable to take into consideration the natural richness of the soil in phosphate of lime, potassa, lime, and nitrogenized substances; for, should one or several of these elements be in abundance already, it is evident that their proportion may be reduced, and even dispensed with, in the chemical manures, without decreasing the yield of the crop.

Q. How can we ascertain what is already in a soil, or what is wanting?

A. Nothing is more easy. It has often been thought that chemical analysis would furnish the proper indications, but we are now obliged to give up this hope. The four substances, to which a soil owes its fertility, are there found in various states: soluble and active, insoluble and inactive. As chemistry has not yet succeeded in making these necessary distinctions, its testimony is not a sufficient guide for agricultural practice. Therefore, we do not recommend chemical analyses, but shall refer to the testimony of simple trials of culture made in small experimental fields, and which every one may perform.

Is it desired to know whether a soil is already provided with nitrogenized materials? Remembering what we have said of plants getting their supply of nitrogen from the air, and of plants drawing theirs from the soil, it is sufficient to sow a handful of wheat upon a small square of ground, which has been manured with the mineral substances only. Without the aid of nitrogenized matter, the mineral manure has scarcely any effect upon wheat. Therefore, if this small square of ground gives a rapid and healthy vegetation and a good crop, we have the proof that the earth had a sufficient supply of nitrogen. Indeed, it cannot be otherwise, since the manure had no nitrogen.

On the other hand, have we to ascertain whether the soil contains the three elements of the mineral manure, phosphate of lime, potassa, and lime? A small plot sown with peas or horse-beans, and without any manure, will give the desired answer. We know the great influence of the mineral manure upon leguminous plants; therefore, if the peas flourish, we may be sure that the soil is provided with phosphate of lime, potassa, and lime.

Two experiments, requiring but a small area of ground, are then sufficient to obtain the indications necessary to a judicious system of culture.

Q. The preceding indications refer only to the case of mineral substances employed together; and there may be lands possessing phosphate of lime, and wanting in available potassa. How shall we ascertain these facts?

A. We may arrive at that knowledge by other similar experiments. For instance, we shall grow wheat in five small plots of ground, contiguous one to the other.

The first plot will receive the complete manure;

The second, the same manure without nitrogen;

The third, a manure without phosphate of lime;

The fourth, a manure without potassa;

The fifth, a manure without sulphate of lime.

The comparison of the five crops will immediately indicate what is wanting in the soil.

Since we have demonstrated that the complete manure is alone able to realize all the conditions necessary to the life of plants, such manures as contain but a portion of the substances of the complete manure, will not give the same results, unless the soil supplies the substance which was wanting.

The variable yield of the different crops, compared with that obtained from the complete manure, will measure the richness of the soil.

We shall here point out how decisive the testimony is, and how absolute the indication. No better example can be taken than the following results obtained in the experimental fields of Vincennes:—

Yield per hectare in 1864	Hectolitres of wheat.
Complete manure	39
" " without lime	37
" " without potassa	28
" " without phosphate	24
" " without nitrogen	13
Land without manure	11

The correlativeness is evident, although the soil in 1864 had not been brought to the same degree of exhaustion to which it has since been purposely reduced; mineral, and especially nitrogenized, substances were already wanting.

Q. This process is ingenious and practical; nevertheless it seems long and complicated, and it is doubtful whether farmers will make such experiments, which, in order to be useful, ought to be made by series of six or seven at a time, and will give indications only after five or six months, or even a year.

A. A moment of consideration will bring a more correct appreciation of the real state of things. Is this method of investigation objectionable by reason of its slowness? All the preceding notions and data permit us readily to foresee the results from all we may observe around us.

For instance, lucern succeeds in one field, and does not thrive in another. From what we have said about the predominating action of potassa in regard to lucern, we have the proof that the deeper layers of the first soil contain potassa, which is wanting in the second.

Peas and horse-beans thrive in another field, whereas lucern is but half successful. This contrast teaches us that the superficial layers, beyond which the roots of peas and beans do not go, are provided with potassa, whereas the subsoil reached by the roots of lucern is without it.

Upon a fourth piece of ground, and with slight manures, wheat has a tendency to become lodged; we know therefore that the soil contains nitrogen. These primary indications greatly simplify the experimental culture, and reduce the series to two or three combinations of manuring substances.

But, notwithstanding their usefulness, these primary indications are not sufficiently precise to be entirely relied upon in practice.

As for the experiments necessary to complete them, he who is afraid of them must possess a religious faith in routine. How is it possible that three or four plots of ground, each with an area of a few square metres (a few square yards), will be in the way of the regular work on a farm?

Agriculture requires decision coupled with judgment, and a constant attention to the smallest details. What would be thought of a mariner who should neglect to consult every day his compass and barometer, and to determine the position of his ship by astronomical observation?

Such a man would be thought little of, and rightly so. Indeed, the more thoroughly we examine agricultural questions, and endeavor to unravel the mysteries of the science, the more we become satisfied that experimental fields will decide the agricultural revolution which has already begun.

The appearance of an experimental field cannot be resisted; in the sight of the contrasts it presents, practical men instinctively feel that there is a power which has been underrated or misapplied. They understand that, instead of unclean manures which are so often without the expected effect, it is infinitely more advantageous to employ less complex substances, having a constant composition, and the proportions of which may be regulated to suit the wants of their fields.

Those who avoid labor, should leave agriculture alone. Husbandry has been called the first of the arts because it is a perpetual combat. It is influenced by everything; rain, sunshine, wind, drought, the nature of the soil, local customs, etc.

In agriculture, common sense is better than wit; and common sense says that, in order to obtain good crops with economy,

5

we must know in advance the natural riches of our lands. No labor should be spared to arrive at this knowledge, which is of the first importance, since without it we proceed only by guesswork, always ending in failure. We should still consider ourselves fortunate, if we were enabled to repair our mistakes by a dearly bought experience.

As a last proof, we refer to the frontispiece, and ask if nature ever spoke to agriculturists in a more striking language.

CHAPTER VI.

The bases for profit in agriculture—Manures are the raw material of the crops—Yields obtained with an expense of 150 to 200 francs of chemical manures per hectare.

QUESTION. Where does the profit in agriculture come from?

ANSWER. From an abundance of manures.

Q. Why?

A. Because manure is the raw material of crops: no manure, no crops; little manure, small crops.

Q. It is true that manure acts upon the yield of crops, but how is it that manure is the cause of profit, since, if the crops are larger, the expenses are also increased?

A. In order to make this truth more apparant, let us figure the cost of a culture of wheat, yielding 14 hectolitres per hectare, which is the average in France.

The expenses of culture are of two kinds, those which are constant and those which are variable.

The *constant expenses* are, the rent of the land, tillage, general expenses, and the seed. Whether the yield be great or small the crop will have to bear all these expenses, since we must always pay for the rent of the land, the taxes, the labor, and the seed.

Therefore, these expenses being constant, the more hectolitres we gather the smaller will be the cost for each hectolitre.

Q. We begin to understand; but before proceeding further, what is the meaning of *general expenses?*

A. They are the expenses of administration, the interest on the capital represented by the buildings on the farm, the taxes, and all such expenses which cannot be classified otherwise, such as the board of the men, fuel, light, repairs, etc., etc.

Q. This is understood. It has been said that the more hectolitres or bushels of wheat per hectare or acre, the less is the cost of production for each hetolitre or bushel. Is it convenient to figure these expenses?

A. We may do so. The following figures correspond to the average culture in France:—

	Per hectare.
Rent	45 francs.
General expenses . .	52 "
Ploughing and tilling .	43 "
Seed	46 "
	186

Q. 186 francs for what productions?

A. 14 hectolitres of grain and 2000 kilogrammes (2 tons) of straw.

Q. What is then the cost of the hectolitre of wheat?

A. 9.70 francs, without calculating the other expenses.

Q. What are these other expenses?

A. They are the cost of manuring and harvesting, which we call *variable expenses*, because, in regard to manures, every one manures as he is able or willing to do, and because the cost of harvesting, transporting, and threshing the grain is variable with the yield of the crop.

Q. We understand this; but how is the account completed?

A. To the 186 francs of constant expenses we should add:—

	Per hectare.
Stable manure . . .	74 francs.
Harvesting, threshing, etc. .	34 "

Or,

Constant expenses . .	186 francs.
Variable expenses . . .	108 "
	294

We should, however, deduct 50 francs from the 294, for the value of the straw, and the total expenses become 244 francs, or 17.43 francs per hectolitre of wheat.

Q. We understand more and more clearly; nevertheless, it seems curious that, by expending more money on manures, the cost of the hectolitre is diminished.

A. We have already said that the crops result from the manures; and it is evident that a field receiving twenty cart loads of stable manure will produce more than if it had received ten only. Let us now put down a few figures:—

With 74 francs of farm-yard manure, the yield is 14 hectolitres of wheat; with 194 francs of the same manure, the yield becomes 31 hectolitres.

In order to produce 31 hectolitres, the taxes are the same; the rent of the ground is not changed; the labor for ploughing and tilling is not increased; and we employ the same amount of seeds. The question may then be summed up as follows:—

Overplus of wheat produced	17 hectolitres.
Increase in expense for manure . . .	120 francs.

The cost of each additional hectolitre of wheat is 7.05 francs, and that of the hectolitre for the whole crop is 11.74 instead of 17.43 francs.

Q. How is it that no account has been taken of the greater expenses of harvesting and threshing, caused by the overplus of 17 hectolitres?

A. Because the overplus of straw covers these expenses, and over, leaving a profit of 29 francs. Therefore the cost of the hectolitre of wheat is reduced to 11.12 francs, as may be seen by a comparison of the two accounts:—

With an expense of 74 francs for stable manure per hectare, we find:—

		Francs.	
Constant expenses	Rent . . .	45	
	General expenses .	52	
	Ploughing, etc. .	43	
	Seeds . . .	46	
		—	186
Variable expenses	Manure . . .	74	
	Harvesting and threshing . .	34	
		—	108
Total expense			294
From which we deduct for straw . .			50
It remains			244

Or, 17.43 francs per hectolitre for a production of 14 hectolitres.

On the other hand, with an expense of 194 francs for stable manure, per hectare, the expenses of production become:—

		Francs.	
Constant expenses:	The same as before		186
Variable expenses	Manure . . .	194	
	Harvesting and threshing . .	60	
		—	254
Total expenses			440
From which we deduct for straw . .			95
It remains			345

Or, 11.12 francs per hectolitre for a production of 31 hectolitres of wheat.

Q. Then, we may grow rich by agriculture?

A. Yes, by thoroughly manuring the soil.

Q. What is to be done when there is not a sufficiency of stable manure?

A. Employ chemical manures. There is the same difference between chemical and stable manures, as between quinine and the bark from which it is extracted.

Q. What is the profit to be derived from the employment of chemical manures alone, or associated with stable manure?

A. From 200 to 300 francs per hectare.

Q. Then it is an entire revolution?

A. Certainly, and one which ought to double the income of France, and allow of the gradual reduction of taxes, at the same time that the people live better. This generation will be the first to profit by it.

APPENDIX.

Ploughing and Preparing the Soil.

In order that stable and chemical manures should produce all their effect, the soil should be well prepared. It has been ascertained that deep ploughing is an essential condition for success in agriculture, and that the mere scraping of the ground is highly objectionable.

We cannot do better, in order to point out the advantages of deep ploughing, than to reproduce the excellent observations of Mr. Schattenmann.

"In the Bas Rhin, and doubtless in many other departments, ploughing is but superficial, and not deeper than from 8 to 12 centimetres (3 to 5 inches). This thickness is evidently insufficient, and should be increased to 30 or 40 centimetres (12 to 16 inches), in order that the plants may thrive. The proportion of mineral substances in the soil is in the ratio of the thickness of the tillable layer, and will be doubled or trebled by deep ploughing. A system of rotation of crops becomes at the same time more easy. The great majority of agriculturists who persist in superficial ploughing, do so for fear of bringing to the surface sterile soils. It is a mistake, since a good subsoil plough allows of the simple stirring and gradual incorporation of the under layers, without bringing them to the surface. Experience has, however, demonstrated that deep ploughing is always advantageous and without the fancied inconveniences. We should fight such prejudices.

"The arable layer, when its thickness is no greater than from 8 to 15 centimetres (3 to 6 inches), is insufficient for the development of the roots of plants, and does not protect them against the influence of an excess of dryness or dampness. As the tendency of plants is to grow as much below as above the surface, it is evident that they cannot expand properly in a thin layer. Therefore, the principal condition of a deeply tilled ground is seldom met with, principally for tobacco, rape-seed (colza), horse-beans, lucern, beets, carrots, and other plants sending their roots deeply into the ground. Even cerealia, which are believed to vegetate at the surface of the soil, will have deep roots in properly prepared ground.

"With an arable layer of 8 to 15 centimetres (3 to 6 inches) thickness, the roots of plants will not acquire their natural growth, and will greatly suffer by the inclemency of the weather. An abundant rain will flood the plants, and when the water escapes over the surface of the field, it will carry away the soluble and more fertilizing substances. By drying, the damp earth will become compact, and will compress the roots, the development of which will thus be hindered. After a long drought, the plants which have their roots near the surface of the soil, finding no dampness, remain stationary, or even perish.

"On the other hand, and in arable layers 30 to 40 centimetres (12 to 16 inches) thick, plants are able to penetrate and to grow properly, and are protected against drought and the inclemency of the weather. An arable layer of this thickness easily absorbs water; during an abundant rain, water penetrates and is drained through the bottom, without carrying away any earth or manure. When the rain ceases, the surface of the soil is quickly dried, and does not become compact, as is the case with too wet grounds. Should a drought take place, the roots of plants which have penetrated sufficiently deep, find there enough dampness to continue to thrive."

Methods of using Chemical Manures.

The employment of chemical manures requires special care. The same as with improved weapons, they show the full measure of their power only to those who understand their use.

Chemical manures should be distributed as regularly as possible, immediately after the last ploughing. The operation resembles broadcast sowing, and is followed by a careful harrowing, which mixes the substances with the soil.

A misty and not windy day is to be preferred. A strong wind is objectionable by causing the loss of part of the manure. When the spreading is performed by hand, it will be more uniform if the manure be mixed with its own volume of fine and dry earth. The mixture is first deposited on the ground, in the shape of small heaps regularly distributed.

In large farms it is preferable to employ the excellent machines at our disposal for spreading pulverulent manures. A good distribution of manures is sufficient to increase the yield of the crop from two to three hectolitres per hectare.

We operate differently for grape-vines: half of the manure is spread in a band 30 centimetres (12 inches) wide, and 20 centimetres (8 inches) distant from the rows of vines. This manure is then buried deep with a spade; and the remainder of the manure is spread at the surface of the ploughed ground.

We may also, by means of the plough, and at the same distance from the rows of vines, dig two parallel trenches 30 centimetres (12 inches) deep, and fill them with one-half of the manure. After covering these trenches, the other half of the manure is distributed over the surface.

Grape-vines should be manured in the fall.

Without repeating what has already been said about the great efficacy of chemical manures, we shall, however, point out how powerful they are for contending against the effects of an unfavorable year.

After a severe and protracted winter, wheat, and, in general, all gramineous plants, are very much enfeebled. With from 100 to 200 kilogrammes of sulphate of ammonia, or 150 to 250 kilogrammes of nitrate of soda mixed with 200 kilogrammes of plaster of Paris, employed as a top dressing at the beginning of March (latitude of Paris), we are enabled to change in a few days the sickly state of the plants, and to insure the crop. The effect of top dressing with chemical manures is extraordinary.

We should, however, be careful, not to wait longer than the latter part of March. Applied in April or May, these top dressings hasten the vegetation so much that straw preponderates, and the grains are small and few.

When, from a rainy fall, the sowing is late, a top dressing of manures may be made immediately after the complete shooting forth of the grain. A windy day should be avoided. With the ordinary stable manure such top dressings are nearly impossible. In the spring, sulphate of ammonia or nitrate of soda is generally sufficient. Nevertheless, we prefer mixing them with 200 kilogrammes of acid phosphate of lime, and 200 kilogrammes of plaster of Paris.

We shall now examine the formulæ of manures adapted to systems of rotation of the principal crops, and shall consider two cases: first, when the chemical manures are employed alone; second, when they are associated with farm-yard manure.

The prices of the substances employed in chemical manures, are on an average (France, 1869):—

Acid phosphate of lime	16	francs per	100 kilog.
Nitrate of potassa . .	62	"	"
Nitrate of soda . . .	35	"	"
Sulphate of ammonia .	45	"	"
Sulphate of lime . . .	2	"	"

FORMULÆ OF MANURES.

Wheat.

	Per Hectare. Quantities. *Kilogrammes.*	Price. *Francs.*
Complete Manure No. 1 . .	**1200**	
That is:		
Acid phosphate of lime . .	400	64.00
Nitrate of potassa . . .	200	124.00
Sulphate of ammonia . .	250	112.50
Sulphate of lime . . .	350	7.00
Total	1200	307.50

Barley, Oats, Rye, Natural Pastures.

	Kilogrammes.	*Francs.*
Complete Manure No. 1 . .	**600**	
That is:		
Acid phosphate of lime . .	200	32.00
Nitrate of potassa . . .	100	62.00
Sulphate of ammonia . .	125	56.25
Sulphate of lime . . .	175	3.50
Total	600	153.75

In the case of natural pastures, the manures may be employed in two different ways, that is, spread entirely in the fall, or 300 kilogrammes (one-half) in the fall, and 300 kilogrammes in the spring after the first cutting.

Hemp, Rape-seed (Colza).

	Per Hectare. Quantities.	Price.
	Kilogrammes.	*Francs.*
Complete Manure No. 1 . .	**1200**	

And should the rape-seed (colza) be followed by wheat:

	Kilogrammes.	*Francs.*
Complete Manure No. 6 . .	**1300**	
That is:		
Acid phosphate of lime . .	400	64.00
Nitrate of potassa . . .	120	74.40
Sulphate of ammonia . .	400	180.00
Sulphate of lime . . .	380	7.60
Total	1300	326.00

Beets, Carrots, Cabbages, Hops, Gardening.

	Kilogrammes.	*Francs.*
Complete Manure No. 2 . .	**1200**	
That is:		
Acid phosphate of lime . .	400	64.00
Nitrate of potassa . . .	200	124.00
Nitrate of soda . . .	300	105.00
Sulphate of lime . . .	300	6.00
Total	1200	299.00

When it is desired to have the greatest yield of beets, it is preferable to substitute for the complete manure No. 2, the complete manure No. 2 *bis*, and still better, the *intense* complete manure No. 2.

	PER HECTARE. Quantities. *Kilogrammes.*	Price. *Francs.*
Complete Manure No. 2 *bis* . .	**1300**	
That is:		
Acid phosphate of lime . .	400	64.00
Nitrate of potassa . . .	200	124.00
Nitrate of soda . . .	400	140.00
Sulphate of lime . . .	300	6.00
Total	1300	334.00

	Kilogrammes.	*Francs.*
Complete Manure (*intense*) **No. 2**	**1600**	
That is:		
Acid phosphate of lime . .	600	96.00
Nitrate of potassa . . .	400	248.00
Nitrate of soda . . .	300	105.00
Sulphate of lime . . .	300	6.00
Total	1600	455.00

Potatoes.

	Kilogrammes.	*Francs.*
Complete Manure No. 3 . .	**1000**	
That is:		
Acid phosphate of lime . .	400	64.00
Nitrate of potassa . . .	300	186.00
Sulphate of lime . . .	300	6.00
Total	1000	256.00

With worn-out soils, it is preferable to employ 1200 kilogrammes of the complete manure No. 2.

Grape-Vines and Small Trees.

	Per Hectare. Quantities. *Kilogrammes.*	Price. *Francs.*
Complete Manure No. 4 . .	**1500**	
That is:		
Acid phosphate of lime . .	600	96.00
Nitrate of potassa . . .	500	310.00
Sulphate of lime . . .	400	8.00
Total	1500	414.00

The complete manure No. 2 gives very good results with grape-vines, and we recommend its use for vineyards giving products of ordinary quality.

Turnips, Rutabagas, Jerusalem Artichokes, Sorgho, Sugar-Cane, Maize.

	Kilogrammes.	*Francs.*
Complete Manure No. 5 . .	**1200**	
That is:		
Acid phosphate of lime . .	600	96.00
Nitrate of potassa . . .	200	124.00
Sulphate of lime . . .	400	8.00
Total	1200	228.00

Beans, Horse-Beans, Peas, Clover, Sainfoin, Vetches, Lucern.

	PER HECTARE. Quantities. *Kilogrammes.*	Price. *Francs.*
Incomplete Manure No. 2 . .	**1000**	
That is:		
Acid phosphate of lime . .	400	64.00
Nitrate of potassa . . .	200	124.00
Sulphate of lime . . .	400	8.00
Total	1000	196.00

Theoretically, this manure should not contain any nitrogen, and the potassa should be in the form of carbonate. The nitrate has been substituted because it is notably cheaper. Moreover, the proportion of nitrogen in the nitrate of potassa amounts only to 28 kilogrammes per hectare, which quantity is entirely too small to be injurious.

When the chemical manures are associated with those from the farm-yard, the preceding formulæ may be reduced one-half.

The farm-yard manure is deeply buried, and the chemical manures are spread over the surface of the soil after the last ploughing.

ROTATION OF CROPS.

First Case.

The chemical manures are employed alone, without admixture of stable manure.

EXCLUSIVE CULTURE OF WHEAT.

FIRST YEAR.

Wheat.

	Per Hectare. Quantities. *Kilogrammes.*	Price. *Francs.*
Complete Manure No. 1 . .	**1200**	
That is:		
Acid phosphate of lime . .	400	64.00
Nitrate of potassa . . .	200	124.00
Sulphate of ammonia . .	250	112.50
Sulphate of lime . . .	350	7.00
Total	1200	307.50

SECOND YEAR.

Wheat.

	Kilogrammes.	*Francs.*
Sulphate of ammonia . .	300	135.00

THIRD YEAR.

Wheat.

	Kilogrammes.	*Francs.*
Complete Manure No. 1 . .	**1200**	
That is:		
Acid phosphate of lime . .	400	64.00
Nitrate of potassa . . .	200	124.00
Sulphate of ammonia . .	250	112.50
Sulphate of lime . . .	350	7.00
Total	1200	307.50

FOURTH YEAR.

Wheat.

	Per Hectare. Quantities. *Kilogrammes.*	Price. *Francs.*
Sulphate of ammonia . .	300	135.00
Expense for four years . .		885.00
Expense for one year . .		221.25

The exclusive culture of wheat unavoidably results in a multiplication of weeds, and to such an extent that, in order to maintain the yield of the crops, it is necessary to go every year to the expense of several hoeings. This inconvenience is avoided by replacing the third crop of wheat by a culture of potatoes or clover. If we decide on the potatoes, we should employ the following manure:—

	Kilogrammes.	*Francs.*
Acid phosphate of lime . .	400	64
Nitrate of potassa . . .	300	186
Sulphate of lime . . .	300	6
Total	1000	256

This change reduces the expenses of the third year 51.50 francs, and the yearly expenses become 208.37 instead of 221.25 francs.

Should clover be preferred, we reduce the proportion of nitrate of potassa down to 200 kilogrammes, and the expense of the third year becomes 196 francs.

ALTERNATE CULTURE OF RAPE-SEED (COLZA) AND WHEAT.

FIRST YEAR.

Rape-Seed (Colza).

	Per Hectare. Quantities. *Kilogrammes.*	Price. *Francs.*
Complete Manure No. 6 . .	**1300**	
That is:		
Acid phosphate of lime . .	400	64.00
Nitrate of potassa . . .	120	74.40
Sulphate of ammonia . .	400	180.00
Sulphate of lime . . .	380	7.60
Total	1300	326.00

SECOND YEAR.

Wheat.

	Kilogrammes.	*Francs.*
Sulphate of ammonia . .	300	135.00
Total expense . . .		461.00
Expense per year . . .		230.50

The straws and capsules of the rape-seed (colza) are burned upon the field, and their ashes are spread upon the soil after the first ploughing. The sulphate of ammonia is distributed after the second ploughing. Instead of burning the straws and capsules of the rape-seed (colza), it is more advantageous to decompose them in the manner indicated in our *Entretiens Agricoles*, vol. i. p. 148.

ROTATION OF FOUR YEARS, COMPRISING:

Potatoes, Wheat, Clover, Wheat.

FIRST YEAR.

Potatoes.

	PER HECTARE. Quantities.	Price.
	Kilogrammes.	*Francs.*
Complete Manure No. 3	**1000**	
That is:		
Acid phosphate of lime	400	64.00
Nitrate of potassa	300	186.00
Sulphate of lime	300	6.00
		256.00

SECOND YEAR.

Wheat.

	Kilogrammes.	*Francs.*
Sulphate of ammonia	300	135.00

THIRD YEAR.

Clover.

	Kilogrammes.	*Francs.*
Incomplete Manure No. 2	**1000**	
That is:		
Acid phosphate of lime	400	64.00
Nitrate of potassa	200	124.00
Sulphate of lime	400	8.00
		196.00

FOURTH YEAR.

Wheat.

	Kilogrammes.	*Francs.*
Sulphate of ammonia	300	135.00

Total expense	722.00
Expense per year	180.50

ROTATION OF FOUR YEARS, COMPRISING:
Beets, Wheat, Clover, Wheat.

FIRST YEAR.
Beets.

	PER HECTARE.	
	Quantities.	Price.
	Kilogrammes.	*Francs.*
Complete Manure No. 2 *bis* . .	**1300**	
That is:		
Acid phosphate of lime . .	400	64.00
Nitrate of potassa . . .	200	124.00
Nitrate of soda . . .	400	140.00
Sulphate of lime . . .	300	6.00
		334.00

SECOND YEAR.
Wheat.

	Kilogrammes.	*Francs.*
Sulphate of ammonia . .	300	135.00

THIRD YEAR.
Clover.

	Kilogrammes.	*Francs.*
Incomplete Manure No. 2 . .	**1000**	
That is:		
Acid phosphate of lime . .	400	64.00
Nitrate of potassa . . .	200	124.00
Sulphate of lime . . .	400	8.00
		196.00

FOURTH YEAR.
Wheat.

	Kilogrammes.	*Francs.*
Sulphate of ammonia . .	300	135.00
Total expense . . .		800.00
Expense per year . .		200.00

ROTATION OF FIVE YEARS, COMPRISING:

Potatoes, Wheat, Clover, Colza, Wheat.

FIRST YEAR.

Potatoes.

	Per Hectare. Quantities.	Price.
	Kilogrammes.	*Francs.*
Complete Manure No. 3 . .	**1000**	
That is:		
Acid phosphate of lime . .	400	64.00
Nitrate of potassa . . .	300	186.00
Sulphate of lime . . .	300	6.00
		256.00

SECOND YEAR.

Wheat.

	Kilogrammes.	*Francs.*
Sulphate of ammonia . .	300	135.00

THIRD YEAR.

Clover.

	Kilogrammes.	*Francs.*
Incomplete Manure No. 2 . .	**1000**	
That is:		
Acid phosphate of lime . .	400	64.00
Nitrate of potassa . . .	200	124.00
Sulphate of lime . . .	400	8.00
		196.00

FOURTH YEAR.

Colza.

	Kilogrammes.	*Francs.*
Sulphate of ammonia . .	400	180.00

FIFTH YEAR.

Wheat.

	Per Hectare. Quantities.	Price.
	Kilogrammes.	*Francs.*
Sulphate of ammonia . .	300	135.00
Total expense . . .		902.00
Expense per year . .		180.40

ROTATION OF TWO YEARS, COMPRISING:

Maize, Wheat.

FIRST YEAR.

Maize.

	Per Hectare. Quantities.	Price.
	Kilogrammes.	*Francs.*
Complete Manure No. 5 . .	**1200**	
That is:		
Acid phosphate of lime . .	600	96.00
Nitrate of potassa . . .	200	124.00
Sulphate of lime . . .	400	8.00
		228.00

SECOND YEAR.

Wheat.

	Kilogrammes.	*Francs.*
Sulphate of ammonia . .	300	135.00
Total expense . . .		363.00
Expense per year . .		181.50

ROTATION OF SIX YEARS, COMPRISING:

Flax, Beets, Wheat, Colza, Wheat, and Oats, Rye, or Barley.

FIRST YEAR.

Flax.

	Per Hectare. Quantities. *Kilogrammes.*	Price. *Francs.*
Incomplete Manure No. 2 . .	**1000**	
That is:		
Acid phosphate of lime . .	400	64.00
Nitrate of potassa . . .	200	124.00
Sulphate of lime . . .	400	8.00
		196.00

SECOND YEAR.

Beets.

	Kilogrammes.	*Francs.*
Complete Manure No. 2 . .	**1200**	
That is:		
Acid phosphate of lime . .	400	64.00
Nitrate of potassa . . .	200	124.00
Nitrate of soda . . .	300	105.00
Sulphate of lime . . .	300	6.00
		299.00

THIRD YEAR.

Wheat.

	Kilogrammes.	*Francs.*
Sulphate of ammonia . .	300	135.00

FOURTH YEAR.

Colza.

	PER HECTARE. Quantities.	Price.
	Kilogrammes.	*Francs.*
Complete Manure No. 6 . . .	**1300**	
That is:		
Acid phosphate of lime . . .	400	64.00
Nitrate of potassa . . .	120	74.40
Sulphate of ammonia . . .	400	180.00
Sulphate of lime . . .	380	7.60
		326.00

FIFTH YEAR.

Wheat.

	Kilogrammes.	*Francs.*
Sulphate of ammonia . . .	300	135.00

SIXTH YEAR.

Oats, Rye, or Barley.

	Kilogrammes.	*Francs.*
Sulphate of ammonia . . .	200	90.00

Total expense . . .	1181.00
Expense per year . .	196.83

ROTATION WITH FODDER PLANTS.

FIRST YEAR.

Wheat.

	Per Hectare. Quantities.	Price.
	Kilogrammes.	*Francs.*
Complete Manure No. 1 . . .	**1200**	
That is:		
Acid phosphate of lime . .	400	64.00
Nitrate of potassa . . .	200	124.00
Sulphate of ammonia . .	250	112.50
Sulphate of lime . . .	350	7.00
		307.50

SECOND YEAR.

Clover.

	Kilogrammes.	*Francs.*
Incomplete Manure No. 2 . .	**1000**	
That is:		
Acid phosphate of lime . .	400	64.00
Nitrate of potassa . . .	200	124.00
Sulphate of lime . . .	400	8.00
		196.00

THIRD YEAR.

Wheat.

	Kilogrammes.	*Francs.*
Sulphate of ammonia . .	300	135.00

FOURTH YEAR.

Vetches, Horse-Beans, Maize mixed.

	Kilogrammes.	*Francs.*
Incomplete Manure No. 2 . .	**1000**	
That is:		
Acid phosphate of lime . .	400	64.00
Nitrate of potassa . . .	200	124.00
Sulphate of lime . . .	400	8.00
		196.00

FIFTH YEAR.

Wheat.

	Per Hectare. Quantities. *Kilogrammes.*	Price. *Francs.*
Sulphate of ammonia . .	300	135.00

SIXTH YEAR.

Vetches, Horse-Beans, Maize mixed.

	Kilogrammes.	*Francs.*
Incomplete Manure No. 2 . .	**1000**	
That is:		
Acid phosphate of lime . .	400	64.00
Nitrate of potassa . . .	200	124.00
Sulphate of lime . . .	400	8.00
		196.00
Total expense . . .		1165.50
Expense per year . .		194.25

MANURES FOR PASTURE (FORAGES).

FIRST YEAR.

	Per Hectare. Quantities. *Kilogrammes.*	Price. *Francs.*
Incomplete Manure No. 2 . .	**1000**	
That is:		
Acid phosphate of lime . .	400	64.00
Nitrate of potassa . . .	200	124.00
Sulphate of lime . . .	400	8.00
		196.00

SECOND YEAR.

	Kilogrammes.	*Francs.*
Sulphate of ammonia . .	300	135.00
Total expense . . .		331.00
Expense per year . .		165.50

Second Case.

The chemical manures are employed as auxiliary to farm-yard manure.

When chemical manures are used as adjuncts to the farm-yard manure, the latter should be considered as equivalent to a certain amount of richness acquired by the soil. Therefore, the chemical manure should be composed principally of those substances which act the more favorably upon the culture of the year.

It then becomes of the highest importance to know the dominant substance for each plant, and the following table will furnish this precious indication:—

Nature of the Cultures.	Dominant.	Corresponding Substances.
Beets, Colza, Wheat, Barley, Oats, Rye, Natural grasses	Nitrogen.	Sulphate of ammonia. Nitrate of soda. Nitrate of potassa.
Peas, Beans, Horse-beans, Clover, Sainfoin, Vetches, Lucern, Flax, Potatoes	Potassa.	Nitrate of potassa. Purified potassa. Silicate of potassa.
Turnips, Rutabagas, Jerusalem artichokes, Maize, Sorghum, Sugar-cane	Phosphate.	Bone-black from sugar-houses. Bone-dust. Superphosphates (acid phosphates).

On the supposition that 50,000 kilogrammes (50 tons) of stable manure are employed per hectare every five years, we now indicate the chemical manures which should be used conjointly.

ROTATION, COMPRISING:

Potatoes, Wheat, Clover, Wheat, Oats.

FIRST YEAR.

Potatoes.

	Per Hectare. Quantities. *Kilogrammes.*	Price. *Francs.*
Stable Manure . . .	**50,000**	

COMPLEMENTARY CHEMICAL MANURES.

	Kilogrammes.	*Francs.*
Incomplete Manure No. 2 . .	**500**	
That is:		
Acid phosphate of lime . .	200	32.00
Nitrate of potassa . . .	100	62.00
Sulphate of lime . . .	200	4.00
		98.00

SECOND YEAR.

Wheat.

	Kilogrammes.	*Francs.*
Sulphate of ammonia . .	200	90.00

THIRD YEAR.

Clover.

	PER HECTARE. Quantities.	Price.
	Kilogrammes.	*Francs.*
Incomplete Manure No. 2 . .	**1,000**	
That is:		
Acid phosphate of lime . .	400	64.00
Nitrate of potassa . . .	200	124.00
Sulphate of lime . . .	400	8.00
		196.00

FOURTH YEAR.

Wheat.

	Kilogrammes.	*Francs.*
Sulphate of ammonia . .	200	90.00

FIFTH YEAR.

Oats.

	Kilogrammes.	*Francs.*
Sulphate of ammonia . .	300	135.00
Total expense		609.00
Expense per year . . .		121.80

ROTATION COMPRISING:

Beets, Wheat, Clover, Wheat, Oats.

FIRST YEAR.

Beets.

	Per Hectare. Quantities.	Price.
	Kilogrammes.	*Francs.*
Stable Manure . . .	**50,000**	

COMPLEMENTARY CHEMICAL MANURES.

	Kilogrammes.	*Francs.*
Complete Manure No. 2 . .	**600**	
That is:		
Acid phosphate of lime . .	200	32.00
Nitrate of potassa . . .	100	62.00
Nitrate of soda . . .	150	52.50
Sulphate of lime . . .	150	3.00
		149.50

SECOND YEAR.

Wheat.

	Kilogrammes.	*Francs.*
Sulphate of ammonia . .	200	90.00

THIRD YEAR.

Clover.

	Kilogrammes.	*Francs.*
Incomplete Manure No. 2 . .	**1,000**	
That is:		
Acid phosphate of lime . .	400	64.00
Nitrate of potassa . . .	200	124.00
Sulphate of lime . . .	400	8.00
		196.00

FOURTH YEAR.

Wheat.

	Kilogrammes.	*Francs.*
Sulphate of ammonia . .	200	90.00

FIFTH YEAR.

Oats.

	Per Hectare.	
	Quantities.	Price.
	Kilogrammes.	*Francs.*
Sulphate of ammonia . .	300	135.00
Total expense		660.50
Expense per year . . .		132.10

ROTATION COMPRISING:

Colza, Beets, Wheat, Clover, Wheat.

FIRST YEAR.

Colza.

	Per Hectare.	
	Quantities.	Price.
	Kilogrammes.	*Francs.*
Stable Manure . . .	**50,000**	

COMPLEMENTARY CHEMICAL MANURES.

	Kilogrammes.	*Francs.*
Sulphate of ammonia . .	300	135.00

SECOND YEAR.

Beets.

	Kilogrammes.	*Francs.*
Incomplete Manure No. 2 (*intense*)	**800**	
That is:		
Acid phosphate of lime . .	300	48.00
Nitrate of potassa . . .	200	124.00
Nitrate of soda . . .	150	52.50
Sulphate of lime . . .	150	3.00
		227.50

THIRD YEAR.

Wheat.

	PER HECTARE.	
	Quantities.	Price.
	Kilogrammes.	*Francs.*
Sulphate of ammonia . .	200	90.00

FOURTH YEAR.

Clover.

	Kilogrammes.	*Francs.*
Incomplete Manure No. 2 . .	**1,000**	
That is:		
Acid phosphate of lime . .	400	64.00
Nitrate of potassa . . .	200	124.00
Sulphate of lime . . .	400	8.00
		196.00

FIFTH YEAR.

Wheat.

	Kilogrammes.	*Francs.*
Sulphate of ammonia . .	200	90.00
Total expense		738.50
Expense per year . . .		147.70

ROTATION OF SIX YEARS, COMPRISING:

Flax, Beets, Wheat, Colza, Wheat, and Oats, Rye or Barley.

FIRST YEAR.

Flax.

	Per Hectare. Quantities. *Kilogrammes.*	Price. *Francs.*
Incomplete Manure No. 2 .	**1,000**	
That is:		
Acid phosphate of lime . .	400	64.00
Nitrate of potassa . . .	200	124.00
Sulphate of lime . . .	400	8.00
		196.00

SECOND YEAR.

Beets.

	Kilogrammes.	*Francs.*
Stable Manure (in the fall) .	**50,000**	
In the spring:		
Complete Manure No. 2, *bis* . .	**650**	
That is:		
Acid phosphate of lime . .	200	32.00
Nitrate of potassa . . .	100	62.00
Nitrate of soda . . .	200	70.00
Sulphate of lime . . .	150	3.00
		167.00

THIRD YEAR.

Wheat.

	Kilogrammes.	*Francs.*
Sulphate of ammonia . .	300	135.00

FOURTH YEAR.

Colza.

	Per Hectare. Quantities. *Kilogrammes.*	Price. *Francs.*
Complete Manure No. 6 .	**1,300**	
That is:		
Acid phosphate of lime . .	400	64.00
Nitrate of potassa . . .	120	74.40
Sulphate of ammonia . .	400	180.00
Sulphate of lime . . .	380	7.60
		326.00

FIFTH YEAR.

Wheat.

	Kilogrammes.	*Francs.*
Sulphate of ammonia . .	300	135.00

SIXTH YEAR.

Oats, Rye, or Barley.

	Kilogrammes.	*Francs.*
Sulphate of ammonia . .	200	90.00
Total expense . . .		1049.00
Expense per year . .		174.83

Instead of beginning by experiments on a large scale, we prefer trying the chemical manures on small experimental fields, at an expense of from 20 to 25 francs (4 to 5 dollars). We will gain by them positive data on the nature of the fertilizing agents which are especially wanting in the soil. We will know, at the same time, the maximum yield which may be obtained.

EXPERIMENTAL FIELDS.

An experimental field may furnish the demonstration of the fundamental data upon which the doctrine of chemical manures is based. It will also indicate the fertilizing substances which are in a soil, and those which are missing.

According to the object in view, its mode of working should be different.

An experimental field for a school, being intended especially for explaining the laws of the production of vegetables, should be worked so as to explain the fundamental data of the doctrine of chemical manures.

For one culture, and three or four combinations of manures, one *are* (about 119.6 square yards) is sufficient. But, if it were possible to set apart three or four *ares* for experiments, it would be proper to repeat the same combinations of manures upon two or three different plants.

EXPERIMENTAL FIELD

FOR A PRIMARY SCHOOL.

Culture of Wheat.

The field will be disposed as follows:

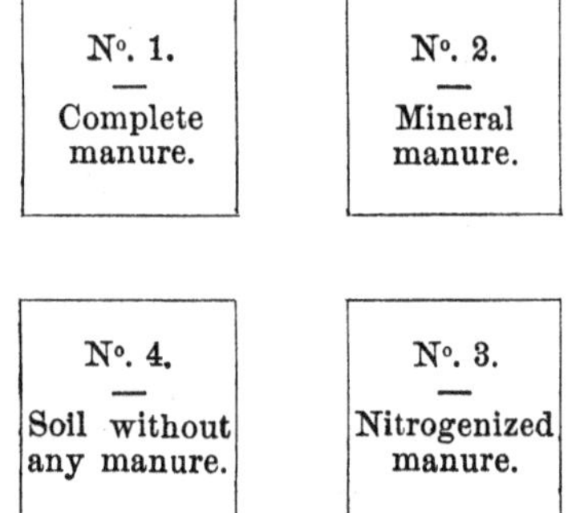

The area of each plot is about 25 square yards.

What is the meaning of these four plots?

Plot No. 1 will demonstrate that splendid crops are obtained with the complete manure.

Plot No. 2 will show that the mixture of the three mineral substances, phosphate of lime, potassa, and lime, gives but meagre results, unless the soil be naturally provided with nitrogen.

Plot No. 3 will prove that nitrogenized matters alone are more powerful than the three mineral substances of No. 2, without being equal in yield to that obtained with the complete manure.

Plot No. 4, without any manure, will determine the natural fertility of the soil.

With another *are* of ground, divided as follows, we may cultivate peas or horse-beans:—

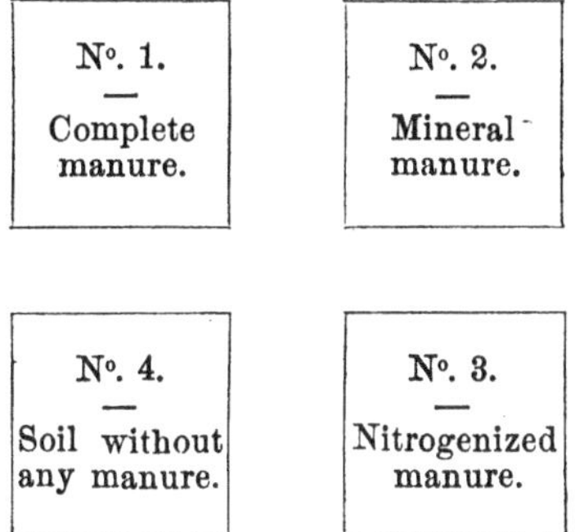

In this case, the crop obtained upon the plot No. 2, which has received only mineral substances, will be at least equal to that of No. 1 with its complete manure, holding nitrogen. It will be a proof that nitrogenized substances are without action upon peas or horse-beans, and that we were perfectly right in separating the plants drawing their nitrogen from the air, from those which extract it from the soil.

This conclusion will be still more fully corroborated by the inferior crop of the plot No. 3, which contains only nitrogenized materials.

Lastly, if it were possible to devote one *are* more of ground to the culture of potatoes, we might demonstrate that the sickness of these tubers may be diminished, if not entirely prevented, by the choice of manures.

This third *are* is disposed as the other two.

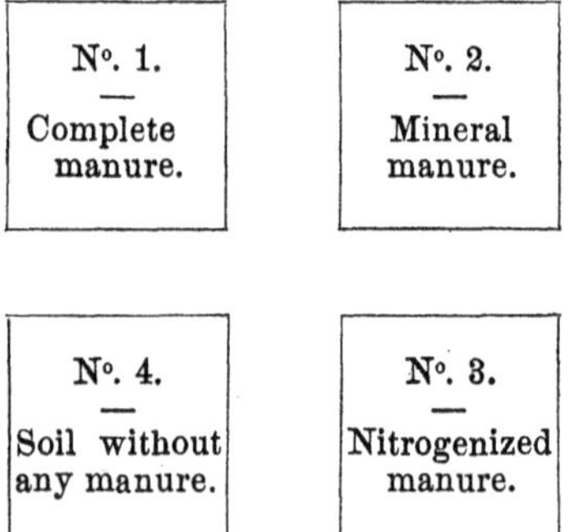

Upon the plot No. 1, the crop will be abundant and healthy.

Upon No. 2, satisfactory and healthy crop.

Upon No. 3, small and sickly crop.

Upon No. 4, small and sickly crop.

These results will prove that the mineral manure contains the dominant substance, and that the wearing out of a soil in mineral elements predisposes, if it does not determine, the sickness.

With an experimental field for three cultures, the following disposition is advantageous:—

Wheat.		*Peas.*		*Potatoes.*	
N°. 1.	N°. 2.	N°. 1.	N°. 2.	N°. 1.	N°. 2.
N°. 4.	N°. 3.	N°. 4.	N°. 3.	N°. 4.	N°. 3.

Each plot is separated from the others by an alley way 1 to 2 metres (1 to 2 yards) wide.

COMPOSITION OF THE MANURES INTENDED FOR THE EXPERIMENTAL FIELDS OF A PRIMARY SCHOOL.

Each plot containing 25 square metres, that is to say, the fourth part of an are, here are the composition and proportions of manure for them:—

(Plot No. 1.)

Complete Manure.*

	Kilogrammes.
Acid phosphate of lime	1.000
Nitrate of potassa	0.500
Sulphate of ammonia	0.625
Sulphate of lime	0.875
Total	3.000

* By doubling the figures of these formulæ, the result will be reckoned in pounds avoirdupois and decimal fractions, which will answer for experimental plots holding each 25 square yards.—*Trans.*

(Plot No. 2.)

Mineral Manure.

	Kilogrammes.
Acid phosphate of lime	1.000
Carbonate of potassa	0.500
Sulphate of lime	0.875
Total	2.375

(Plot No. 3.)

Nitrogenized Manure.

	Kilogrammes.
Sulphate of ammonia	1.375

The above manures will be employed during the first year. During the second year, the plots Nos. 1 and 3 will receive a top dressing of 0.750 kilogramme of sulphate of ammonia; Nos. 2 and 4 will receive nothing. The regular quantities will be employed for the third year.

EXPERIMENTAL FIELD

FOR THE ANALYSIS OF THE SOIL.

When an experimental field is intended for the analysis of the useful substances contained in a soil, it should be subdivided into a greater number of plots.

On a large farm it will be wise to have several such fields, and one of them, the principal one, should contain all the plants of a rotation.

The position of the experimental field is very important, and we should, as far as practicable, choose a piece of ground which, by its exposure, degree of fertility, and nature, is a good average of that portion of the farm. The principal field should contain ten plots of one are each, and separated by alleys 1 metre wide.

We have said that all, or at least the principal, cultures of the rotation should be made, and this requires at least two or three parallel series of culture. Among the plants which are to be preferred, if all cannot be tried, we shall state wheat, colza or beets, and peas or beans. Wheat and peas will indicate the nature of the superficial layers of the soil, and that of the subsoil or deeper layers will be demonstrated by colza or beets. These two data are of the greatest importance when we desire to cultivate with intelligence and profit.

We have also said that each plant should be submitted to ten different modes of manuring upon ten separated plots; we now give these manures:—

WHEAT No. 1. Stable manure, 60 tons per hectare.
No. 2. Stable manure, 30 tons per hectare.
No. 3. Complete chemical manure (*intense.*)
No. 4. Complete chemical manure.
No. 5. Chemical manure without nitrogen.
No. 6. Chemical manure without phosphate of lime.
No. 7. Chemical manure without potassa.
No. 8. Chemical manure without lime.
No. 9. Nitrogenized manure without mineral substances.
No. 10. Natural soil without any manure.

On large farms, one field is not sufficient, because there may be great variations in the composition of the soil of different parts of the property. We should therefore multiply the trials, but on a smaller scale. One *are*, divided into four parts, is sufficient for these auxiliary fields, each part receiving one of the following manures:—

No. 1. Complete chemical manure.
No. 2. Chemical manure without nitrogen.
No. 3. Nitrogen manure without mineral substances.
No. 4. The natural soil without any manure.

A few plots of ground, set apart for these experiments, will not interfere with the regular farming operations, and they will point out, for each subdivision of the property, the precise time when nitrogenized or mineral manures are needed.

There may be persons who will feel alarmed at the prospect of so many trials; we shall answer them that, in every farm where the chemical manures are employed, the owner, tenant, or manager is always proud of his experimental fields, delights in showing them to his visitors, and, after a little hesitation, finishes by regulating the composition and proportion of chemical manures from their teachings.

Let us now consider the preparation of the manures intended for the analysis of the soil in experimental fields. The proportions indicated are intended for one *hectare;* but we have found out by practice that plots of one *are* are convenient and sufficient.

SERIES FOR WHEAT.

(Plot No. 1.)

	Kilogrammes.
Farm-yard Manure . .	60,000 (60 tons.)

(Plot No. 2.)

	Kilogrammes.
Farm-yard Manure . .	30,000 (30 tons.)

Complete Manure, intense.

(Plot No. 3.)

	PER HECTARE.	
	Quantities.	Price.
	Kilogrammes.	*Francs.*
Acid phosphate of lime . .	600	96.00
Nitrate of potassa . . .	400	248.00
Sulphate of ammonia . .	250	112.50
Sulphate of lime . . .	350	7.00
		463.50

Complete Manure.

(Plot No. 4.)

	Kilogrammes.	*Francs.*
Acid phosphate of lime . .	400	64.00
Nitrate of potassa . . .	200	124.00
Sulphate of ammonia . .	250	112.50
Sulphate of lime . . .	350	7.00
		307.50

Manure without Nitrogen.

(Plot No. 5.)

	Kilogrammes.	*Francs.*
Acid phosphate of lime . .	400	64.00
Carbonate of potassa . .	150	120.00
Sulphate of lime . .	350	7.00
		191.00

Manure without Phosphate.

(Plot No. 6.)

	Per Hectare. Quantities.	Price.
	Kilogrammes.	*Francs.*
Nitrate of potassa . . .	200	124.00
Sulphate of ammonia . .	250	112.50
Sulphate of lime . . .	350	7.00
		243.50

Manure without Potassa.

(Plot No. 7.)

	Kilogrammes.	*Francs.*
Acid phosphate of lime . .	400	64.00
Sulphate of ammonia . .	400	180.00
Sulphate of lime . . .	200	4.00
		248.00

Manure without Lime.

(Plot No. 8.)

	Kilogrammes.	*Francs.*
Precipitated phosphate of lime	400	64.00
Nitrate of potassa . . .	200	124.00
Sulphate of ammonia . .	250	112.50
		300.50

Manure without Minerals.

(Plot No. 9.)

	Kilogrammes.	*Francs.*
Sulphate of ammonia . .	400	180

SERIES FOR BEETS.

(Plot No. 1.)

	Kilogrammes.
Farm-yard Manure . .	60,000 (60 tons.)

(Plot No. 2.)

	Kilogrammes.
Farm-yard Manure . .	30,000 (30 tons.)

Complete Manure, intense.

(Plot No. 3.)

	Per Hectare.	
	Quantities.	Price.
	Kilogrammes.	*Francs.*
Acid phosphate of lime . .	600	96.00
Nitrate of potassa . . .	400	248.00
Nitrate of soda . . .	300	105.00
Sulphate of lime . . .	300	6.00
		455.00

Complete Manure.

(Plot No. 4.)

	Kilogrammes.	*Francs.*
Acid phosphate of lime . .	400	64.00
Nitrate of potassa . . .	200	124.00
Nitrate of soda . . .	300	105.00
Sulphate of lime . . .	300	6.00
		299.00

Manure without Nitrogen.

(Plot No. 5.)

	Kilogrammes.	*Francs.*
Acid phosphate of lime . .	400	64.00
Carbonate of potassa . .	150	120.00
Sulphate of lime . . .	350	7.00
		191.00

Manure without Phosphate.
(Plot No. 6.)

	Per Hectare. Quantities.	Price.
	Kilogrammes.	*Francs.*
Nitrate of potassa . . .	200	124.00
Nitrate of soda . . .	300	105.00
Sulphate of lime . . .	300	6.00
		235.00

Manure without Potassa.
(Plot No. 7.)

	Kilogrammes.	*Francs.*
Acid phosphate of lime . .	400	64.00
Nitrate of soda . . .	450	157.50
Sulphate of lime . . .	350	7.00
		228.50

Manure without Lime.
(Plot No. 8.)

	Kilogrammes.	*Francs.*
Precipitated phosphate of lime	400	64.00
Nitrate of potassa . . .	200	124.00
Nitrate of soda . . .	300	105.00
		293.00

Manure without Minerals.
(Plot No. 9.)

	Kilogrammes.	*Francs.*
Nitrate of soda . . .	450	157.50

In order that the indications given by experimental fields should be thoroughly useful, in regard to the real nature of a soil, the ground should not have been manured for several years, otherwise the yields of the different plots will present no marked differences. The contrasts obtained at Vincennes are produced only after two or three years of culture. But such an occurrence is none the less instructive, since it demonstrates that the soil is provided with the elements of the complete manure.

This indication is capital in practice, because we are sure that, with such a soil, we may temporarily use incomplete manures, or simply the dominant substances for a given culture. It is the manner of obtaining the greatest yield with the minimum of expense.

NOTE.—In large experimental fields the nitrate of potassa will be cheaper than the carbonate, and the proportions of the former will be found in previous formulæ for a given crop. But, for small experimental plots of a few square yards, it is preferable to use carbonate of potassa.

Manure without lime means a manure without sulphate of lime, or any other lime compound, else than the tribasic phosphate of lime (precipitated phosphate), which is obtained by adding to the solution of soluble acid phosphate of lime, just enough lime to saturate the excess of phosphoric acid.

The other phosphates without lime are too expensive.—*Trans.*

VOCABULARY

OF

CHEMICAL MANURES.

NITROGENIZED SUBSTANCES.

WE designate under this head the products of vegetable or animal origin which contain nitrogen.

Blood, albumen, horn-waste, woollen-waste, excrements, litters, seed-cakes, etc., are nitrogenized materials. In order to act upon the vegetation, such substances should be decomposed in the soil; and without this previous decomposition they possess no action upon plants.

When nitrogenized substances become decomposed, a part of their nitrogen is transformed into ammonia or a nitrate. On this account, we classify among the nitrogenized products convenient for agricultural purposes:—

Sulphate of ammonia,
Nitrate of potassa,
And nitrate of soda.

These substances are chemical salts, holding nitrogen as a constituent part. In the sulphate of ammonia the nitrogen belongs to the ammonia. In the nitrates of potassa and soda, the nitrogen is found in the acid of the salt.

SULPHATE OF AMMONIA.

This salt is composed of sulphuric acid and ammonia, as follows:—

Sulphuric acid	60.60
Ammonia	25.76
Water	13.64
	100.00

And, as the composition of ammonia is

Nitrogen	14
Hydrogen	3
	17

It follows that chemically pure sulphate of ammonia contains 21.21 per cent. of nitrogen. The commercial salts yield at most 20 per cent. of nitrogen.

Ammonia is extracted from the liquors of cesspools, and from the watery liquid condensed during the distillation of bituminous coal in gas works. But it appears that eventually the most important supply of ammonia will be derived from volcanoes, when they have reached that stage of quietness when steam only is disengaged.

In 1866 (in France) the sulphate of ammonia was worth 35 francs per 100 kilogrammes. At the present time (1869) its value is 45 francs; but there is every reason to believe that it will be lowered in price.

NITRATE OF SODA.

Nitrate of soda is formed of nitric acid and soda. Its exact composition is:—

Nitric acid	63.53
Soda	36.47
	100.00

And, as nitric acid itself is formed of

Nitrogen	14
Oxygen	40
	54

It follows that chemically pure nitrate of soda contains 16.4 per cent. of nitrogen. The commercial article holds only from 14 to 15 per cent. of nitrogen. Nitrate of soda comes from Peru, where it exists in the form of compact masses, mixed with sand and common salt.

The earthquakes which took place this year (1869) on the coast of Peru, have reduced the exportation of this product, and its price rose to 40 francs per 100 kilogrammes, instead of

35 francs which was its cost the preceding year.

NITRATE OF POTASSA.

This salt, also known under the names of *nitre* or *saltpetre*, is formed of nitric acid and potassa. Its composition is:—

Nitric acid	53.41
Potassa	46.59
	100.00

And, with the ratio of 14 parts of nitrogen to 54 parts of nitric acid, it results that the proportion of nitrogen is 13.8 per cent. of the chemically pure nitrate of potassa. That in the commercial salt varies from 12 to 13 per cent.

Nitrate of potassa is obtained by the decomposition, under large open sheds, of materials of animal origin mixed with earths holding clay and limestone, and which are afterwards lixiviated in order to extract the nitre. This salt, for a long time, was produced from old building materials. It is now manufactured by decomposing chloride of potassium with nitrate of soda, and the resulting products are chloride of sodium (common salt) and nitrate of potassa, which are easily separated one from the other by crystallization.

Nitrate of potassa, of all potassic compounds, is that which should be preferred for agricultural purposes. Its price, at the present time (1869, in France), is 62 francs per 100 kilogrammes.

PHOSPHATE OF LIME.

Quite a number of different products are known under the denomination of phosphate of lime. For a long time the only phosphate of lime used in agriculture was that of bones, which is combined with a certain proportion of carbonate of lime. Now the greater portion of the phosphates for manures comes from the mineral kingdom, where inexhaustible deposits are found.

All the phosphates are formed of phosphoric acid and lime, and the phosphoric acid itself is composed of phosphorus and oxygen, as follows:—

Phosphorus	31
Oxygen	40
	71

In phosphates, phosphoric acid is the active compound. Chemists represent phosphoric acid by the symbol PhO^5 or PO^5.

PhO^5 or 71 of phosphoric acid being constant in composition, we know three principal combinations of phosphate of lime.

The *First* is $PhO^5 \left\{ \begin{array}{l} CaO \\ 2HO \end{array} \right.$ which is composed of—

Phosphoric acid	60.68
Lime (CaO)	23.93
Water (2HO)	15.39
	100.00

This product is the acid phosphate of lime. In the arts, it is prepared by the reaction of sulphuric acid upon bones, or mineral phosphates. The acid phosphate is therefore mixed with sulphate of lime, and, in that shape, is called superphosphate of lime.

It contains from 15 to 18 per cent. of phosphoric acid, and is sold at 16 francs per 100 kilogrammes (France, 1869).

The *Second* phosphate is represented by the formula $PhO^5 \left\{ \begin{array}{l} 2CaO \\ HO, \end{array} \right.$ or

Phosphoric acid	52.20
Lime (2CaO)	41.18
Water (HO)	6.62
	100.00

It differs from the former in the proportion of lime, which is greater. This phosphate possesses remarkable properties, which it is useless to mention, since it is not found in the trade.

The *Third* phosphate has for symbol PhO^5, 3CaO, and its composition is:—

Phosphoric acid	45.81
Lime	54.19
	100.00

We see that the proportion of phosphoric acid, in these three phosphates, is represented by—

1	60.68 per cent.
2	52.20 "
3	45.81 "

The last, and poorest in phosphoric acid, is the bone phosphate. It is also naturally found in the form of nodules, and of apatite.

In the nodular state, the phosphate is mixed with from 40 to 50 per cent. of foreign matters, and is sold, powdered, at 6 francs per 100 kilogrammes.

Calcined and powdered bones are worth 16 francs. In regard to apatite, it is so compact that it cannot be employed in the natural state, and is reserved for the manufacture of acid phosphate of lime.

SULPHATE OF LIME.

Sulphate of lime is nothing else but plaster of Paris, that is, a combination of sulphuric acid and lime, which is naturally found in the hydrated state, and forms large deposits. Its composition is:—

Sulphuric acid	46.51
Lime	32.56
Water	20.93
	100.00

Heated at a temperature of 120° to 130° C., it loses its water and becomes anhydrous, or plaster.

We advise the employment of the anhydrous sulphate of lime, which, in that state, is worth 2 francs per 100 kilogrammes.

INDEX.

ACID phosphate of lime, 30, 36, 38
Agriculture, objects of, 13
  the demands of, 48, 49
Air, nitrogen extracted from the, by certain plants, 22
Air, the, 14
Ammonia, sulphate of, 106
Analysis of soils, experimental fields for, 97
Animal substances holding assimilable nitrogen, 28, 29
Artichokes, manure for, 70
Assimilability of manures, 25

BARREN or exhausted soils, 17
Barley, 23
  oats, rye, natural pastures, manure for, 67
Basis of profit, 80
Beans, manure for, 71
Beets, 23, 37
  and potatoes, nitrates for, 28
  experimental series for, 102
  manure for, 40, 68
Bone black, 30
  dust, 30

CABBAGES, manure for, 68
  Carbonate and sulphate of lime, 33
Cerealia, 29
  nitrogen for, 38
Chalk, 33
Chemical manure, 17
  manures auxiliary to farm manure, 83
    modes of using, 62–66
Clover, 23, 24
  manure for, 71
Complete manure, 17, 39
  and mineral manure, when used, 22
Constituent parts of manure, action of, 34
Colza, manure for, 68
Corn, Indian, manure for, 70
Crops, rotation of, 73–90
  substances necessary for obtaining, 17, 18

DECOMPOSITION, effects of light, heat, etc., in producing, 27
  necessary in manures, 26
Deep ploughing, 59–62

EXHAUSTED or barren soils, 17
Exhaustion of soil, 15
Expenses and profits with chemical manures, 41

Expenses—
constant, 51
general, 52
Experimental fields for the analysis of soils, 97
fields, 43–50, 91–104
importance of, 91
of Vincennes, 19, 46, 104

FALLOW land, 27
Farm-yard manure, 16, 17
Farm-yard manure, foreign substances in, 17
Fertility of the soil, preservation of, 15
Foreign substances in farm-yard manure, 17
Formation of plants, 13, 14
Formulæ of manures, 67-71

GARDENING, manure for, 68
Germination, 14
Grape-vines, manure for, 70
manuring, 63

HEMP, manure for, 68
Hops, manure for, 68
Horn and woollen rags, 25
Horse-beans, 24
manure for, 71

INDIAN corn, manure for, 70

LABORATORY experiments as to nitrogen, 23
Lime, 16, 18, 26, 36
phosphate of, 109

Lime—
sulphate of, 111
Lucern, manure for, 71

MAIZE, manure for, 40, 71
Manure, action of the constituent parts of, 34
Manure, complete, 17, 39
for beets, 40
for maize, 40
for potatoes, 40
mineral, 20
the raw material of crops, 51, 57
Manures, assimilability of, 25
composition of, for experimental fields of a primary school, 95
decomposition necessary in, 26
formulæ of, 67–71
spreading, 63
the bases of profit in agriculture, 50–57
Manuring, 16
Mineral manure, 20
and complete manure also used, 22

NATURAL pastures, manure for, 67
Nitrate of potassa, 28, 29, 31, 32, 36, 38, 108
soda, 36, 127
Nitre, 31
Nitrogen, assimilable, 28, 29
aptitude of certain plants for extracting from the air, 21
compounds, best, 31
furnished by the air and the soil, 23
in crops, 22
Nitrogenized matter, 16, 18, 25, 35

Nitrogenized—
substances, 105
Nitrogen not extracted from the air in sufficient quantity by most crops, 22
of nitrate of potassa, 32
profits in, 37
Nitrogenous matter the dominant substance in manures of cerealia, 38
Nourishment of plants, 14

OATS, barley, rye, and natural pastures, manure for, 67

PEAS, manure for, 71
beans, lucern, clover, 21
Phosphate of lime, 16, 18, 26, 30, 31, 36, 38, 109
Plants, formation of, 13, 14
having an aptitude for extracting nitrogen from the air, 21
nourishment of, 14
Plaster of Paris, 38
Ploughing and preparing the soil, 59, 62
superficial, 59
Potassa, 16, 18, 26, 31, 35
nitrate and carbonate of, 104
nitrate of, 108
of wood-ashes, 32
Potassas, refined, 32
Potatoes and beets, nitrates for, 28
manure for, 40, 69,
Preparing the soil, 59–62
Primary school, experimental field for, 92
Profit, basis of, 50, 57
Profit—
and expenses with chemical manures, 41
in nitrogen, 37
Poudrette, 28

RAPE-SEED, 23, 29
manure for, 68
Refined potassas, 32
Restoration of the soil, 15
Roots of plants, development of, 60
Rotation of crops, 24, 41, 73, 90
Rye, 23
oats, barley, and natural pastures, manure for, 67

SAINFOIN, manure for, 71
Saltpetre, 31
Schattenmann, Mr. 59
Seed, growth from, 14
Skin and leather, 26
Soda, nitrate of, 109
Soil, exhaustion of, 15
experimental field for analysis of, 97
preparing, 59–62
preservation of the fertility of, 15
restoration of, 15
the, 14
Soils, chemistry unable to give the elements in, 42
elements in, 42
Solubility necessary in manures, 25, 26, 27, 33
Sorgho, manure for, 70
Substances for formation of plants, 14
Sugar-cane, 38
manure for, 70

Sulphate and carbonate of lime, 33
of ammonia, 28, 106
lime, 30, 36, 38, 111
Sulphuric acid, 31
Superficial ploughing, 59

TOP dressing with chemical manures, 65
Trees, small, manure for, 70
Turnips, manure for, 70

UNFAVORABLE year, effects of chemical manures on, 64
Using chemical manures, 62–66

VEGETABLES, certain, action of nitrogenized matter upon, 35
Vegetables—
certain, action of phosphate of lime on, 36
certain, action of potassa upon, 35
which thrive upon mineral manure, 32
Vetches, manure for, 71
Vincennes, experimental fields of, 19, 46, 104
Vocabulary of chemical manures, 105

WHEAT, 23, 24
experimental series for, 100
experiments with, 44, 46
manure for, 67
Wood-ashes, potassa of, 32
Woollen rags and horn, 25

CATALOGUE
OF
PRACTICAL AND SCIENTIFIC BOOKS,
PUBLISHED BY
HENRY CAREY BAIRD,
INDUSTRIAL PUBLISHER,
No. 406 WALNUT STREET,
PHILADELPHIA.

☞ Any of the Books comprised in this Catalogue will be sent by mail, free of postage, at the publication price.

☞ MY NEW AND ENLARGED CATALOGUE, 95 pages 8vo., with full descriptions of Books, will be sent, free of postage, to any one who will favor me with his address.

ARMENGAUD, AMOUROUX, AND JOHNSON.—THE PRACTICAL DRAUGHTSMAN'S BOOK OF INDUSTRIAL DESIGN, AND MACHINIST'S AND ENGINEER'S DRAWING COMPANION: Forming a complete course of Mechanical Engineering and Architectural Drawing. From the French of M. Armengaud the elder, Prof. of Design in the Conservatoire of Arts and Industry, Paris, and MM. Armengaud the younger and Amouroux, Civil Engineers. Rewritten and arranged, with additional matter and plates, selections from and examples of the most useful and generally employed mechanism of the day. By WILLIAM JOHNSON, Assoc. Inst. C. E., Editor of "The Practical Mechanic's Journal." Illustrated by 50 folio steel plates and 50 wood-cuts. A new edition, 4to. . $10 00

ARLOT.—A COMPLETE GUIDE FOR COACH PAINTERS. Translated from the French of M. ARLOT, Coach Painter; late Master Painter for eleven years with M. Ehrler, Coach Manufacturer, Paris. With important American additions . . $1 25

ARROWSMITH.—PAPER-HANGER'S COMPANION: A Treatise in which the Practical Operations of the Trade are Systematically laid down: with Copious Directions Preparatory to Papering; Preventives against the Effect of Damp on Walls; the Various Cements and Pastes adapted to the Several Purposes of the Trade; Observations and Directions for the Panelling and Ornamenting of Rooms, &c. By JAMES ARROWSMITH. 12mo., cloth $1 25

BAIRD.—THE AMERICAN COTTON SPINNER, AND MANAGER'S AND CARDER'S GUIDE:

A Practical Treatise on Cotton Spinning; giving the Dimensions and Speed of Machinery, Draught and Twist Calculations, etc.; with notices of recent Improvements: together with Rules and Examples for making changes in the sizes and numbers of Roving and Yarn. Compiled from the papers of the late ROBERT H. BAIRD. 12mo. . . . $1 50

BAKER.—LONG-SPAN RAILWAY BRIDGES:

Comprising Investigations of the Comparative Theoretical and Practical Advantages of the various Adopted or Proposed Type Systems of Construction; with numerous Formulæ and Tables. By B. Baker. 12mo. $2 00

BAKEWELL.—A MANUAL OF ELECTRICITY—PRACTICAL AND THEORETICAL:

By F. C. BAKEWELL, Inventor of the Copying Telegraph. Second Edition. Revised and enlarged. Illustrated by numerous engravings. 12mo. Cloth . . . . .

BEANS.—A TREATISE ON RAILROAD CURVES AND THE LOCATION OF RAILROADS:

By E. W. BEANS, C. E. 12mo. . . . $2 00

BLENKARN.—PRACTICAL SPECIFICATIONS OF WORKS EXECUTED IN ARCHITECTURE, CIVIL AND MECHANICAL ENGINEERING, AND IN ROAD MAKING AND SEWERING:

To which are added a series of practically useful Agreements and Reports. By JOHN BLENKARN. Illustrated by fifteen large folding plates. 8vo. $9 00

BLINN.—A PRACTICAL WORKSHOP COMPANION FOR TIN, SHEET-IRON, AND COPPER-PLATE WORKERS:

Containing Rules for Describing various kinds of Patterns used by Tin, Sheet-iron, and Copper-plate Workers; Practical Geometry; Mensuration of Surfaces and Solids; Tables of the Weight of Metals, Lead Pipe, etc.; Tables of Areas and Circumferences of Circles; Japans, Varnishes, Lackers, Cements, Compositions, etc. etc. By LEROY J. BLINN, Master Mechanic. With over One Hundred Illustrations. 12mo. $2 50

BOOTH.—MARBLE WORKER'S MANUAL:

Containing Practical Information respecting Marbles in general, their Cutting, Working, and Polishing; Veneering of Marble; Mosaics; Composition and Use of Artificial Marble, Stuccos, Cements, Receipts, Secrets, etc. etc. Translated from the French by M. L. BOOTH. With an Appendix concerning American Marbles. 12mo., cloth . . $1 50

BOOTH AND MORFIT.—THE ENCYCLOPEDIA OF CHEMISTRY, PRACTICAL AND THEORETICAL:

Embracing its application to the Arts, Metallurgy, Mineralogy, Geology, Medicine, and Pharmacy. By JAMES C. BOOTH, Melter and Refiner in the United States Mint, Professor of Applied Chemistry in the Franklin Institute, etc., assisted by CAMPBELL MORFIT, author of "Chemical Manipulations," etc. Seventh edition. Complete in one volume, royal 8vo., 978 pages, with numerous wood-cuts and other illustrations. $5 00

BOWDITCH.—ANALYSIS, TECHNICAL VALUATION, PURIFICATION, AND USE OF COAL GAS:

By Rev. W. R. BOWDITCH. Illustrated with wood engravings. 8vo. $6 50

BOX.—PRACTICAL HYDRAULICS:

A Series of Rules and Tables for the use of Engineers, etc. By THOMAS BOX. 12mo. $2 50

BUCKMASTER.—THE ELEMENTS OF MECHANICAL PHYSICS:

By J. C. BUCKMASTER, late Student in the Government School of Mines; Certified Teacher of Science by the Department of Science and Art; Examiner in Chemistry and Physics in the Royal College of Preceptors; and late Lecturer in Chemistry and Physics of the Royal Polytechnic Institute. Illustrated with numerous engravings. In one vol. 12mo. . $1 50

BULLOCK.—THE AMERICAN COTTAGE BUILDER:

A Series of Designs, Plans, and Specifications, from $200 to to $20,000 for Homes for the People; together with Warming, Ventilation, Drainage, Painting, and Landscape Gardening. By JOHN BULLOCK, Architect, Civil Engineer, Mechanician, and Editor of "The Rudiments of Architecture and Building," etc. Illustrated by 75 engravings. In one vol. 8vo. $3 50

BULLOCK.—THE RUDIMENTS OF ARCHITECTURE AND BUILDING:

For the use of Architects, Builders, Draughtsmen, Machinists, Engineers, and Mechanics. Edited by JOHN BULLOCK, author of "The American Cottage Builder." Illustrated by 250 engravings. In one volume 8vo. . . . $3 50

BURGH.—PRACTICAL ILLUSTRATIONS OF LAND AND MARINE ENGINES:

Showing in detail the Modern Improvements of High and Low Pressure, Surface Condensation, and Super-heating, together with Land and Marine Boilers. By N. P. BURGH, Engineer. Illustrated by twenty plates, double elephant folio, with text. $21 00

BURGH.—PRACTICAL RULES FOR THE PROPORTIONS OF MODERN ENGINES AND BOILERS FOR LAND AND MARINE PURPOSES.

By N. P. BURGH, Engineer. 12mo. . . . $2 00

BURGH.—THE SLIDE-VALVE PRACTICALLY CONSIDERED:

By N. P. BURGH, author of "A Treatise on Sugar Machinery," "Practical Illustrations of Land and Marine Engines," "A Pocket-Book of Practical Rules for Designing Land and Marine Engines, Boilers," etc. etc. etc. Completely illustrated. 12mo. $2 00

BYRN.—THE COMPLETE PRACTICAL BREWER:

Or, Plain, Accurate, and Thorough Instructions in the Art of Brewing Beer, Ale, Porter, including the Process of making Bavarian Beer, all the Small Beers, such as Root-beer, Ginger-pop, Sarsaparilla-beer, Mead, Spruce beer, etc. etc. Adapted to the use of Public Brewers and Private Families. By M. LA FAYETTE BYRN, M. D. With illustrations. 12mo. $1 25

BYRN.—THE COMPLETE PRACTICAL DISTILLER:

Comprising the most perfect and exact Theoretical and Practical Description of the Art of Distillation and Rectification; including all of the most recent improvements in distilling apparatus; instructions for preparing spirits from the numerous vegetables, fruits, etc.; directions for the distillation and preparation of all kinds of brandies and other spirits, spirituous and other compounds, etc. etc.; all of which is so simplified that it is adapted not only to the use of extensive distillers, but for every farmer, or others who may wish to engage in the art of distilling By M. LA FAYETTE BYRN, M. D. With numerous engravings. In one volume, 12mo. $1 50

BYRNE.—POCKET BOOK FOR RAILROAD AND CIVIL ENGINEERS:

Containing New, Exact, and Concise Methods for Laying out Railroad Curves, Switches, Frog Angles and Crossings; the Staking out of work; Levelling; the Calculation of Cuttings; Embankments; Earth-work, etc. By OLIVER BYRNE. Illustrated, 18mo., full bound $1 75

BYRNE.—THE HANDBOOK FOR THE ARTISAN, MECHANIC, AND ENGINEER:

By OLIVER BYRNE. Illustrated by 185 Wood Engravings. 8vo. $5 00

BYRNE.—THE ESSENTIAL ELEMENTS OF PRACTICAL MECHANICS:

For Engineering Students, based on the Principle of Work. By OLIVER BYRNE. Illustrated by Numerous Wood Engravings, 12mo. $3 63

BYRNE.—THE PRACTICAL METAL-WORKER'S ASSISTANT:

Comprising Metallurgic Chemistry; the Arts of Working all Metals and Alloys; Forging of Iron and Steel; Hardening and Tempering; Melting and Mixing; Casting and Founding; Works in Sheet Metal; the Processes Dependent on the Ductility of the Metals; Soldering; and the most Improved Processes and Tools employed by Metal-Workers. With the Application of the Art of Electro-Metallurgy to Manufacturing Processes; collected from Original Sources, and from the Works of Holtzapffel, Bergeron, Leupold, Plumier, Napier, and others. By OLIVER BYRNE. A New, Revised, and improved Edition, with Additions by John Scoffern, M. B , William Clay, Wm. Fairbairn, F. R. S., and James Napier. With Five Hundred and Ninety-two Engravings; Illustrating every Branch of the Subject. In one volume, 8vo. 652 pages . $7 00

BYRNE.—THE PRACTICAL MODEL CALCULATOR:

For the Engineer, Mechanic, Manufacturer of Engine Work, Naval Architect, Miner, and Millwright. By OLIVER BYRNE. 1 volume, 8vo., nearly 600 pages $4 50

BEMROSE.—MANUAL OF WOOD CARVING: With Practical Illustrations for Learners of the Art, and Original and Selected designs. By WILLIAM BEMROSE, Jr. With an Introduction by LLEWELLYN JEWITT, F. S. A., etc. With 128 Illustrations. 4to., cloth $3 00

BAIRD.—PROTECTION OF HOME LABOR AND HOME PRODUCTIONS NECESSARY TO THE PROSPERITY OF THE AMERICAN FARMER:

By HENRY CAREY BAIRD. 8vo., paper 10

BAIRD.—THE RIGHTS OF AMERICAN PRODUCERS, AND THE WRONGS OF BRITISH FREE TRADE REVENUE REFORM.

By HENRY CAREY BAIRD. (1870) 5

BAIRD.—SOME OF THE FALLACIES OF BRITISH-FREE-TRADE REVENUE-REFORM.

Two Letters to Prof. A. L. Perry, of Williams College, Mass. By HENRY CAREY BAIRD. (1871.) Paper 5

BAIRD.—STANDARD WAGES COMPUTING TABLES:

An Improvement in all former Methods of Computation, so arranged that wages for days, hours, or fractions of hours, at a specified rate per day or hour, may be ascertained at a glance. By T. SPANGLER BAIRD. Oblong folio $5 00

BAUERMAN.—TREATISE ON THE METALLURGY OF IRON.

Illustrated. 12mo. $2 50

BICKNELL'S VILLAGE BUILDER.

55 large plates. 4to. $10 00

BISHOP.—A HISTORY OF AMERICAN MANUFACTURES:

From 1608 to 1866; exhibiting the Origin and Growth of the Principal Mechanic Arts and Manufactures, from the Earliest Colonial Period to the Present Time; By J. LEANDER BISHOP, M. D., EDWARD YOUNG, and EDWIN T. FREEDLEY. Three vols. 8vo.,

$10 00

BOX.—A PRACTICAL TREATISE ON HEAT AS APPLIED TO THE USEFUL ARTS:

For the use of Engineers, Architects, etc. By THOMAS BOX, author of "Practical Hydraulics." Illustrated by 14 plates, containing 114 figures. 12mo. $4 25

CABINET MAKER'S ALBUM OF FURNITURE:

Comprising a Collection of Designs for the Newest and Most Elegant Styles of Furniture. Illustrated by Forty-eight Large and Beautifully Engraved Plates. In one volume, oblong

$5 00

CHAPMAN.—A TREATISE ON ROPE-MAKING:

As practised in private and public Rope-yards, with a Description of the Manufacture, Rules, Tables of Weights, etc., adapted to the Trade; Shipping, Mining, Railways, Builders, etc. By ROBERT CHAPMAN. 24mo. $1 50

CRAIK.—THE PRACTICAL AMERICAN MILLWRIGHT AND MILLER.

Comprising the Elementary Principles of Mechanics, Mechanism, and Motive Power, Hydraulics and Hydraulic Motors, Mill-dams, Saw Mills, Grist Mills, the Oat Meal Mill, the Barley Mill, Wool Carding, and Cloth Fulling and Dressing, Wind Mills, Steam Power, &c. By DAVID CRAIK, Millwright. Illustrated by numerous wood engravings, and five folding plates. 1 vol. 8vo. $5 00

CAMPIN.—A PRACTICAL TREATISE ON MECHANICAL ENGINEERING:

Comprising Metallurgy, Moulding, Casting, Forging, Tools, Workshop Machinery, Mechanical Manipulation, Manufacture of Steam-engines, etc. etc. With an Appendix on the Analysis of Iron and Iron Ores. By FRANCIS CAMPIN, C. E. To which are added, Observations on the Construction of Steam Boilers, and Remarks upon Furnaces used for Smoke Prevention; with a Chapter on Explosions. By R. Armstrong, C. E., and John Bourne. Rules for Calculating the Change Wheels for Screws on a Turning Lathe, and for a Wheel-cutting Machine. By J. LA NICCA. Management of Steel, including Forging, Hardening, Tempering, Annealing, Shrinking, and Expansion. And the Case-hardening of Iron. By G. EDE. 8vo. Illustrated with 29 plates and 100 wood engravings. $6 00

CAMPIN.—THE PRACTICE OF HAND-TURNING IN WOOD, IVORY, SHELL, ETC.:

With Instructions for Turning such works in Metal as may be required in the Practice of Turning Wood, Ivory, etc. Also an Appendix on Ornamental Turning. By FRANCIS CAMPIN, with Numerous Illustrations, 12mo., cloth . . . $3 00

CAPRON DE DOLE.—DUSSAUCE.—BLUES AND CARMINES OF INDIGO.

A Practical Treatise on the Fabrication of every Commercial Product derived from Indigo. By FELICIEN CAPRON DE DOLE. Translated, with important additions, by Professor H. DUSSAUCE. 12mo.

CAREY.—THE WORKS OF HENRY C. CAREY:

CONTRACTION OR EXPANSION? REPUDIATION OR RESUMPTION? Letters to Hon. Hugh McCulloch. 8vo. 38

FINANCIAL CRISES, their Causes and Effects. 8vo. paper 25

HARMONY OF INTERESTS; Agricultural, Manufacturing, and Commercial. 8vo., paper $1 00
Do. do. cloth $1 50

LETTERS TO THE PRESIDENT OF THE UNITED STATES. Paper $1 00

MANUAL OF SOCIAL SCIENCE. Condensed from Carey's "Principles of Social Science." By KATE MCKEAN. 1 vol. 12mo. $2 25

MISCELLANEOUS WORKS: comprising "Harmony of Interests," "Money," "Letters to the President," "French and American Tariffs," "Financial Crises," "The Way to Outdo England without Fighting Her," "Resources of the Union," "The Public Debt," "Contraction or Expansion," "Review of the Decade 1857—'67," "Reconstruction," etc. etc. 1 vol. 8vo., cloth $4 50

MONEY: A LECTURE before the N. Y. Geographical and Statistical Society. 8vo., paper 25

PAST, PRESENT, AND FUTURE. 8vo. $2 50

PRINCIPLES OF SOCIAL SCIENCE. 3 volumes 8vo., cloth $10 00

REVIEW OF THE DECADE 1857—'67. 8vo., paper 50

RECONSTRUCTION: INDUSTRIAL, FINANCIAL, AND POLITICAL. Letters to the Hon. Henry Wilson, U. S. S. 8vo paper 50

THE PUBLIC DEBT, LOCAL AND NATIONAL. How to provide for its discharge while lessening the burden of Taxation. Letter to David A. Wells, Esq., U. S. Revenue Commission. 8vo., paper 25

THE RESOURCES OF THE UNION. A Lecture read, Dec. 1865, before the American Geographical and Statistical Society, N. Y., and before the American Association for the Advancement of Social Science, Boston . . . 50

THE SLAVE TRADE, DOMESTIC AND FOREIGN; Why it Exists, and How it may be Extinguished. 12mo., cloth $1 50

LETTERS ON INTERNATIONAL COPYRIGHT. (1867.) Paper 50

REVIEW OF THE FARMERS' QUESTION. (1870.) Paper 25

RÉSUMPTION! HOW IT MAY PROFITABLY BE BROUGHT ABOUT. (1869.) 8vo., paper 50

REVIEW OF THE REPORT OF HON. D. A. WELLS, Special Commissioner of the Revenue. (1869.) 8vo., paper 50

SHALL WE HAVE PEACE? Peace Financial and Peace Political. Letters to the President Elect. (1868.) 8vo., paper 50

THE FINANCE MINISTER AND THE CURRENCY, AND THE PUBLIC DEBT. (1868.) 8vo., paper . . 50

THE WAY TO OUTDO ENGLAND WITHOUT FIGHTING HER. Letters to Hon. Schuyler Colfax. (1865.) 8vo., paper $1 00

WEALTH! OF WHAT DOES IT CONSIST? (1870.) Paper 25

CAMUS.—A TREATISE ON THE TEETH OF WHEELS:
Demonstrating the best forms which can be given to them for the purposes of Machinery, such as Mill-work and Clock-work. Translated from the French of M. CAMUS. By JOHN I. HAWKINS. Illustrated by 40 plates. 8vo. $3 00

COXE.—MINING LEGISLATION.
A paper read before the Am. Social Science Association. By ECKLEY B. COXE. Paper 20

COLBURN.—THE GAS-WORKS OF LONDON:
Comprising a sketch of the Gas-works of the city, Process of Manufacture, Quantity Produced, Cost, Profit, etc. By ZERAH COLBURN. 8vo., cloth 75

COLBURN.—THE LOCOMOTIVE ENGINE:
Including a Description of its Structure, Rules for Estimating its Capabilities, and Practical Observations on its Construction and Management. By ZERAH COLBURN. Illustrated. A new edition. 12mo. $1 25

COLBURN AND MAW.—THE WATER-WORKS OF LONDON:
Together with a Series of Articles on various other Water-works. By ZERAH COLBURN and W. MAW. Reprinted from "Engineering." In one volume, 8vo. . . $4 00

DAGUERREOTYPIST AND PHOTOGRAPHER'S COMPANION:
12mo., cloth $1 25

DIRCKS.—PERPETUAL MOTION:

Or Search for Self-Motive Power during the 17th, 18th, and 19th centuries. Illustrated from various authentic sources in Papers, Essays, Letters, Paragraphs, and numerous Patent Specifications, with an Introductory Essay by HENRY DIRCKS, C. E. Illustrated by numerous engravings of machines. 12mo., cloth $3 50

DIXON.—THE PRACTICAL MILLWRIGHT'S AND ENGINEER'S GUIDE:

Or Tables for Finding the Diameter and Power of Cogwheels; Diameter, Weight, and Power of Shafts; Diameter and Strength of Bolts, etc. etc. By THOMAS DIXON. 12mo., cloth. $1 50

DUNCAN.—PRACTICAL SURVEYOR'S GUIDE:

Containing the necessary information to make any person, of common capacity, a finished land surveyor without the aid of a teacher. By ANDREW DUNCAN. Illustrated. 12mo., cloth. $1 25

DUSSAUCE.—A NEW AND COMPLETE TREATISE ON THE ARTS OF TANNING, CURRYING, AND LEATHER DRESSING:

Comprising all the Discoveries and Improvements made in France, Great Britain, and the United States. Edited from Notes and Documents of Messrs. Sallerou, Grouvelle, Duval, Dessables, Labarraque, Payen, René, De Fontenelle, Malapeyre, etc. etc. By Prof. H. DUSSAUCE, Chemist. Illustrated by 212 wood engravings. 8vo. $10 00

DUSSAUCE.—A GENERAL TREATISE ON THE MANUFACTURE OF SOAP, THEORETICAL AND PRACTICAL:

Comprising the Chemistry of the Art, a Description of all the Raw Materials and their Uses. Directions for the Establishment of a Soap Factory, with the necessary Apparatus, Instructions in the Manufacture of every variety of Soap, the Assay and Determination of the Value of Alkalies, Fatty Substances, Soaps, etc. etc. By PROFESSOR H. DUSSAUCE. With an Appendix, containing Extracts from the Reports of the International Jury on Soaps, as exhibited in the Paris Universal Exposition, 1867, numerous Tables, etc. etc. Illustrated by engravings. In one volume 8vo. of over 800 pages $10 00

DUSSAUCE.—PRACTICAL TREATISE ON THE FABRICATION OF MATCHES, GUN COTTON, AND FULMINATING POWDERS.

By Professor H. DUSSAUCE. 12mo. $3 00

DUSSAUCE.—A PRACTICAL GUIDE FOR THE PERFUMER:
Being a New Treatise on Perfumery the most favorable to the Beauty without being injurious to the Health, comprising a Description of the substances used in Perfumery, the Formulæ of more than one thousand Preparations, such as Cosmetics, Perfumed Oils, Tooth Powders, Waters, Extracts, Tinctures, Infusions, Vinaigres, Essential Oils, Pastels, Creams, Soaps, and many new Hygienic Products not hitherto described. Edited from Notes and Documents of Messrs. Debay, Lunel, etc. With additions by Professor H. DUSSAUCE, Chemist. 12mo. $3 00

DUSSAUCE.—A GENERAL TREATISE ON THE MANUFACTURE OF VINEGAR, THEORETICAL AND PRACTICAL.
Comprising the various methods, by the slow and the quick processes, with Alcohol, Wine, Grain, Cider, and Molasses, as well as the Fabrication of Wood Vinegar, etc. By Prof. H. DUSSAUCE. 12mo. $5 00

DUPLAIS.—A COMPLETE TREATISE ON THE DISTILLATION AND MANUFACTURE OF ALCOHOLIC LIQUORS:
From the French of M. DUPLAIS. Translated and Edited by M. MCKENNIE, M D. Illustrated by numerous large plates and wood engravings of the best apparatus calculated for producing the finest products. In one vol. royal 8vo. $10 00

☞ This is a treatise of the highest scientific merit and of the greatest practical value, surpassing in these respects, as well as in the variety of its contents, any similar volume in the English language.

DE GRAFF.—THE GEOMETRICAL STAIR-BUILDERS' GUIDE:
Being a Plain Practical System of Hand-Railing, embracing all its necessary Details, and Geometrically Illustrated by 22 Steel Engravings; together with the use of the most approved principles of Practical Geometry. By SIMON DE GRAFF, Architect. 4to. $5 00

DYER AND COLOR-MAKER'S COMPANION:
Containing upwards of two hundred Receipts for making Colors, on the most approved principles, for all the various styles and fabrics now in existence; with the Scouring Process, and plain Directions for Preparing, Washing-off, and Finishing the Goods. In one vol. 12mo. $1 25

EASTON.—A PRACTICAL TREATISE ON STREET OR HORSE-POWER RAILWAYS:

Their Location, Construction, and Management; with General Plans and Rules for their Organization and Operation; together with Examinations as to their Comparative Advantages over the Omnibus System, and Inquiries as to their Value for Investment; including Copies of Municipal Ordinances relating thereto. By ALEXANDER EASTON, C. E. Illustrated by 23 plates, 8vo., cloth $2 00

FORSYTH.—BOOK OF DESIGNS FOR HEAD-STONES, MURAL, AND OTHER MONUMENTS:

Containing 78 Elaborate and Exquisite Designs. By FORSYTH. 4to., cloth $5 00

*** This volume, for the beauty and variety of its designs, has never been surpassed by any publication of the kind, and should be in the hands of every marble-worker who does fine monumental work.

FAIRBAIRN.—THE PRINCIPLES OF MECHANISM AND MACHINERY OF TRANSMISSION:

Comprising the Principles of Mechanism, Wheels, and Pulleys, Strength and Proportions of Shafts, Couplings of Shafts, and Engaging and Disengaging Gear. By WILLIAM FAIRBAIRN, Esq., C. E., LL. D., F. R. S., F. G. S., Corresponding Member of the National Institute of France, and of the Royal Academy of Turin; Chevalier of the Legion of Honor, etc. etc. Beautifully illustrated by over 150 wood-cuts. In one volume 12mo. $2 50

FAIRBAIRN.—PRIME-MOVERS:

Comprising the Accumulation of Water-power; the Construction of Water-wheels and Turbines; the Properties of Steam; the Varieties of Steam-engines and Boilers and Wind-mills. By WILLIAM FAIRBAIRN, C. E., LL. D., F. R. S., F. G. S. Author of "Principles of Mechanism and the Machinery of Transmission." With Numerous Illustrations. In one volume. (In press.)

GILBART.—A PRACTICAL TREATISE ON BANKING:

By JAMES WILLIAM GILBART. To which is added: THE NATIONAL BANK ACT AS NOW IN FORCE. 8vo. . . . $4 50

GESNER.—A PRACTICAL TREATISE ON COAL, PETROLEUM, AND OTHER DISTILLED OILS.

By ABRAHAM GESNER, M..D., F. G. S. Second edition, revised and enlarged. By GEORGE WELTDEN GESNER, Consulting Chemist and Engineer. Illustrated. 8vo. . . . $3 50

GOTHIC ALBUM FOR CABINET MAKERS:
Comprising a Collection of Designs for Gothic Furniture. Illustrated by twenty-three large and beautifully engraved plates. Oblong $3 00

GRANT.—BEET-ROOT SUGAR AND CULTIVATION OF THE BEET:
By E. B. GRANT. 12mo. $1 25

GREGORY.—MATHEMATICS FOR PRACTICAL MEN:
Adapted to the Pursuits of Surveyors, Architects, Mechanics, and Civil Engineers. By OLINTHUS GREGORY. 8vo., plates, cloth $3 00

GRISWOLD.—RAILROAD ENGINEER'S POCKET COMPANION.
Comprising Rules for Calculating Deflection Distances and Angles, Tangential Distances and Angles, and all Necessary Tables for Engineers; also the art of Levelling from Preliminary Survey to the Construction of Railroads, intended Expressly for the Young Engineer, together with Numerous Valuable Rules and Examples. By W. GRISWOLD. 12mo., tucks. $1 75

GUETTIER.—METALLIC ALLOYS:
Being a Practical Guide to their Chemical and Physical Properties, their Preparation, Composition, and Uses. Translated from the French of A. GUETTIER, Engineer and Director of Founderies, author of "La Fouderie en France," etc. etc. By A. A. FESQUET, Chemist and Engineer. In one volume, 12mo. $3 00

HATS AND FELTING:
A Practical Treatise on their Manufacture. By a Practical Hatter. Illustrated by Drawings of Machinery, &c., 8vo. $1 25

HAY.—THE INTERIOR DECORATOR:
The Laws of Harmonious Coloring adapted to Interior Decorations: with a Practical Treatise on House-Painting. By D. R. HAY, House-Painter and Decorator. Illustrated by a Diagram of the Primary, Secondary, and Tertiary Colors. 12mo. $2 25

HUGHES.—AMERICAN MILLER AND MILLWRIGHT'S ASSISTANT:
By WM. CARTER HUGHES. A new edition. In one volume, 12mo. $1 50

HUNT.—THE PRACTICE OF PHOTOGRAPHY.

By Robert Hunt, Vice-President of the Photographic Society, London. With numerous illustrations. 12mo., cloth . 75

HURST.—A HAND-BOOK FOR ARCHITECTURAL SURVEYORS:

Comprising Formulæ useful in Designing Builders' work, Table of Weights, of the materials used in Building, Memoranda connected with Builders' work, Mensuration, the Practice of Builders' Measurement, Contracts of Labor, Valuation of Property, Summary of the Practice in Dilapidation, etc. etc. By J. F. Hurst, C. E. 2d edition, pocket-book form, full bound $2 50

JERVIS.—RAILWAY PROPERTY:

A Treatise on the Construction and Management of Railways; designed to afford useful knowledge, in the popular style, to the holders of this class of property; as well as Railway Managers, Officers, and Agents. By John B. Jervis, late Chief Engineer of the Hudson River Railroad, Croton Aqueduct, &c. One vol. 12mo., cloth $2 00

JOHNSON.—A REPORT TO THE NAVY DEPARTMENT OF THE UNITED STATES ON AMERICAN COALS:

Applicable to Steam Navigation and to other purposes. By Walter R. Johnson. With numerous illustrations. 607 pp. 8vo., ... $10 00

JOHNSTON.—INSTRUCTIONS FOR THE ANALYSIS OF SOILS, LIMESTONES, AND MANURES.

By J. W. F. Johnston. 12mo. 35

KEENE.—A HAND-BOOK OF PRACTICAL GAUGING,

For the Use of Beginners, to which is added a Chapter on Distillation, describing the process in operation at the Custom House for ascertaining the strength of wines. By James B. Keene, of H. M. Customs. 8vo. . . . $1 25

KENTISH.—A TREATISE ON A BOX OF INSTRUMENTS,

And the Slide Rule; with the Theory of Trigonometry and Logarithms, including Practical Geometry, Surveying, Measuring of Timber, Cask and Malt Gauging, Heights, and Distances. By THOMAS KENTISH. In one volume. 12mo. . . $1 25

KOBELL.—ERNI.—MINERALOGY SIMPLIFIED:

A short method of Determining and Classifying Minerals, by means of simple Chemical Experiments in the Wet Way. Translated from the last German Edition of F. VON KOBELL, with an Introduction to Blowpipe Analysis and other additions. By HENRI ERNI, M. D., Chief Chemist, Department of Agriculture, author of "Coal Oil and Petroleum." In one volume. 12mo. $2 50

LANDRIN.—A TREATISE ON STEEL:

Comprising its Theory, Metallurgy, Properties, Practical Working, and Use. By M. H. C. LANDRIN, Jr., Civil Engineer. Translated from the French, with Notes, by A. A. FESQUET, Chemist and Engineer. With an Appendix on the Bessemer and the Martin Processes for Manufacturing Steel, from the Report of ABRAM S. HEWITT, United States Commissioner to the Universal Exposition, Paris, 1867. 12mo. . . $3 00

LARKIN.—THE PRACTICAL BRASS AND IRON FOUNDER'S GUIDE.

A Concise Treatise on Brass Founding, Moulding, the Metals and their Alloys, etc.; to which are added Recent Improvements in the Manufacture of Iron, Steel by the Bessemer Process, etc. etc. By JAMES LARKIN, late Conductor of the Brass Foundry Department in Reany, Neafie & Co.'s Penn Works, Philadelphia. Fifth edition, revised, with extensive Additions. In one volume. 12mo. $2 25

LEAVITT.—FACTS ABOUT PEAT AS AN ARTICLE OF FUEL:
With Remarks upon its Origin and Composition, the Localities in which it is found, the Methods of Preparation and Manufacture, and the various Uses to which it is applicable; together with many other matters of Practical and Scientific Interest. To which is added a chapter on the Utilization of Coal Dust with Peat for the Production of an Excellent Fuel at Moderate Cost, especially adapted for Steam Service. By H. T. LEAVITT. Third edition. 12mo. . . . $1 75

LEROUX.—A PRACTICAL TREATISE ON THE MANUFACTURE OF WORSTEDS AND CARDED YARNS:
Translated from the French of CHARLES LEROUX, Mechanical Engineer, and Superintendent of a Spinning Mill. By Dr. H. PAINE, and A. A. FESQUET. Illustrated by 12 large plates. In one volume 8vo. $5 00

LESLIE (MISS).—COMPLETE COOKERY:
Directions for Cookery in its Various Branches. By MISS LESLIE. 60th edition. Thoroughly revised, with the addition of New Receipts. In 1 vol. 12mo., cloth . . $1 50

LESLIE (MISS). LADIES' HOUSE BOOK:
a Manual of Domestic Economy. 20th revised edition. 12mo., cloth $1 25

LESLIE (MISS).—TWO HUNDRED RECEIPTS IN FRENCH COOKERY.
12mo. 50

LIEBER.—ASSAYER'S GUIDE:
Or, Practical Directions to Assayers, Miners, and Smelters, for the Tests and Assays, by Heat and by Wet Processes, for the Ores of all the principal Metals, of Gold and Silver Coins and Alloys, and of Coal, etc. By OSCAR M. LIEBER. 12mo., cloth $1 25

LOVE.—THE ART OF DYEING, CLEANING, SCOURING, AND FINISHING:
On the most approved English and French methods; being Practical Instructions in Dyeing Silks, Woollens, and Cottons, Feathers, Chips, Straw, etc.; Scouring and Cleaning Bed and Window Curtains, Carpets, Rugs, etc.; French and English Cleaning, etc. By THOMAS LOVE. Second American Edition, to which are added General Instructions for the Use of Aniline Colors. 8vo. 5 00

MAIN AND BROWN.—QUESTIONS ON SUBJECTS CONNECTED WITH THE MARINE STEAM-ENGINE:

And Examination Papers; with Hints for their Solution. By THOMAS J. MAIN, Professor of Mathematics, Royal Naval College, and THOMAS BROWN, Chief Engineer, R. N. 12mo., cloth $1 50

MAIN AND BROWN.—THE INDICATOR AND DYNAMOMETER:

With their Practical Applications to the Steam-Engine. By THOMAS J. MAIN, M. A. F. R., Ass't Prof. Royal Naval College, Portsmouth, and THOMAS BROWN, Assoc. Inst. C. E., Chief Engineer, R. N., attached to the R. N. College. Illustrated. From the Fourth London Edition. 8vo. $1 50

MAIN AND BROWN.—THE MARINE STEAM-ENGINE.

By THOMAS J. MAIN, F. R. Ass't S. Mathematical Professor at Royal Naval College, and THOMAS BROWN, Assoc. Inst. C. E. Chief Engineer, R. N. Attached to the Royal Naval College. Authors of "Questions Connected with the Marine Steam-Engine," and the "Indicator and Dynamometer." With numerous Illustrations. In one volume 8vo. $5 00

MARTIN.—SCREW-CUTTING TABLES, FOR THE USE OF MECHANICAL ENGINEERS:

Showing the Proper Arrangement of Wheels for Cutting the Threads of Screws of any required Pitch; with a Table for Making the Universal Gas-Pipe Thread and Taps. By W. A. MARTIN, Engineer. 8vo. 50

MILES—A PLAIN TREATISE ON HORSE-SHOEING.

With Illustrations. By WILLIAM MILES, author of "The Horse's Foot"

MOLESWORTH.—POCKET-BOOK OF USEFUL FORMULÆ AND MEMORANDA FOR CIVIL AND MECHANICAL ENGINEERS.

By GUILFORD L. MOLESWORTH, Member of the Institution of Civil Engineers, Chief Resident Engineer of the Ceylon Railway. Second American from the Tenth London Edition. In one volume, full bound in pocket-book form $2 00

MOORE.—THE INVENTOR'S GUIDE:

Patent Office and Patent Laws: or, a Guide to Inventors, and a Book of Reference for Judges, Lawyers, Magistrates, and others. By J G. MOORE. 12mo., cloth $1 25

NAPIER.—A MANUAL OF ELECTRO-METALLURGY:

Including the Application of the Art to Manufacturing Processes. By JAMES NAPIER. Fourth American, from the Fourth London edition, revised and enlarged. Illustrated by engravings. In one volume, 8vo. $2 00

NAPIER.—A SYSTEM OF CHEMISTRY APPLIED TO DYEING:
By James Napier, F. C. S. A New and Thoroughly Revised Edition, completely brought up to the present state of the Science, including the Chemistry of Coal Tar Colors. By A. A. Fesquet, Chemist and Engineer. With an Appendix on Dyeing and Calico Printing, as shown at the Paris Universal Exposition of 1867, from the Reports of the International Jury, etc. Illustrated. In one volume 8vo., 400 pages $5 00

NEWBERY.—GLEANINGS FROM ORNAMENTAL ART OF EVERY STYLE;
Drawn from Examples in the British, South Kensington, Indian, Crystal Palace, and other Museums, the Exhibitions of 1851 and 1862, and the best English and Foreign works. In a series of one hundred exquisitely drawn Plates, containing many hundred examples. By Robert Newbery. 4to. $15 00

NICHOLSON.—A MANUAL OF THE ART OF BOOK-BINDING:
Containing full instructions in the different Branches of Forwarding, Gilding, and Finishing. Also, the Art of Marbling Book-edges and Paper. By James B. Nicholson. Illustrated. 12mo. cloth $2 25

NORRIS.—A HAND-BOOK FOR LOCOMOTIVE ENGINEERS AND MACHINISTS:
Comprising the Proportions and Calculations for Constructing Locomotives; Manner of Setting Valves; Tables of Squares, Cubes, Areas, etc. etc. By Septimus Norris, Civil and Mechanical Engineer. New edition. Illustrated, 12mo., cloth $2 00

NYSTROM.—ON TECHNOLOGICAL EDUCATION AND THE CONSTRUCTION OF SHIPS AND SCREW PROPELLERS:
For Naval and Marine Engineers. By John W. Nystrom, late Acting Chief Engineer U. S. N. Second edition, revised with additional matter. Illustrated by seven engravings. 12mo. $2 50

O'NEILL.—A DICTIONARY OF DYEING AND CALICO PRINTING:
Containing a brief account of all the Substances and Processes in use in the Art of Dyeing and Printing Textile Fabrics: with Practical Receipts and Scientific Information. By Charles O'Neill, Analytical Chemist; Fellow of the Chemical Society of London; Member of the Literary and Philosophical Society of Manchester; Author of "Chemistry of Calico Printing and Dyeing." To which is added An Essay on Coal Tar Colors and their Application to

Dyeing and Calico Printing. By A. A. FESQUET, Chemist and Engineer. With an Appendix on Dyeing and Calico Printing, as shown at the Exposition of 1867, from the Reports of the International Jury, etc. In one volume 8vo., 491 pages . . $6 00

OSBORN.—THE METALLURGY OF IRON AND STEEL:

Theoretical and Practical: In all its Branches; With Special Reference to American Materials and Processes. By H. S. OSBORN, LL. D., Professor of Mining and Metallurgy in Lafayette College, Easton, Pa. Illustrated by 230 Engravings on Wood, and 6 Folding Plates. 8vo., 972 pages $10 00

OSBORN.—AMERICAN MINES AND MINING:

Theoretically and Practically Considered. By Prof. H. S. OSBORN, Illustrated by numerous engravings. 8vo. (*In preparation.*)

PAINTER, GILDER, AND VARNISHER'S COMPANION:

Containing Rules and Regulations in everything relating to the Arts of Painting, Gilding, Varnishing, and Glass Staining, with numerous useful and valuable Receipts; Tests for the Detection of Adulterations in Oils and Colors, and a statement of the Diseases and Accidents to which Painters, Gilders, and Varnishers are particularly liable, with the simplest methods of Prevention and Remedy. With Directions for Graining, Marbling, Sign Writing, and Gilding on Glass. To which are added COMPLETE INSTRUCTIONS FOR COACH PAINTING AND VARNISHING. 12mo., cloth, $1 50

PALLETT.—THE MILLER'S, MILLWRIGHT'S, AND ENGINEER'S GUIDE.

By HENRY PALLETT. Illustrated. In one vol. 12mo. . $3 00

PERKINS.—GAS AND VENTILATION.

Practical Treatise on Gas and Ventilation. With Special Relation to Illuminating, Heating, and Cooking by Gas. Including Scientific Helps to Engineer-students and others. With illustrated Diagrams. By E. E. PERKINS. 12mo., cloth . . . $1 25

PERKINS AND STOWE.—A NEW GUIDE TO THE SHEET-IRON AND BOILER PLATE ROLLER:

Containing a Series of Tables showing the Weight of Slabs and Piles to Produce Boiler Plates, and of the Weight of Piles and the Sizes of Bars to Produce Sheet-iron; the Thickness of the Bar Gauge in Decimals; the Weight per foot, and the Thickness on the Bar or Wire Gauge of the fractional parts of an inch; the Weight per sheet, and the Thickness on the Wire Gauge of Sheet-iron of various dimensions to weigh 112 lbs. per bundle; and the conversion of Short Weight into Long Weight, and Long Weight into Short. Estimated and collected by G. H. PERKINS and J. G. STOWE $2 50

PHILLIPS AND DARLINGTON.—RECORDS OF MINING AND METALLURGY:

Or, Facts and Memoranda for the use of the Mine Agent and Smelter. By J. ARTHUR PHILLIPS, Mining Engineer, Graduate of the Imperial School of Mines, France, etc., and JOHN DARLINGTON. Illustrated by numerous engravings. In one vol. 12mo. . $2 00

PRADAL, MALEPEYRE, AND DUSSAUCE.—A COMPLETE TREATISE ON PERFUMERY:

Containing notices of the Raw Material used in the Art, and the Best Formulæ. According to the most approved Methods followed in France, England, and the United States. By M. P. PRADAL, Perfumer-Chemist, and M. F. MALEPEYRE. Translated from the French, with extensive additions, by Prof. H. DUSSAUCE. 8vo. $10

PROTEAUX.—PRACTICAL GUIDE FOR THE MANUFACTURE OF PAPER AND BOARDS.

By A. PROTEAUX, Civil Engineer, and Graduate of the School of Arts and Manufactures, Director of Thiers's Paper Mill, 'Puy-de-Dômé. With additions, by L. S. LE NORMAND. Translated from the French, with Notes, by HORATIO PAINE, A. B., M. D. To which is added a Chapter on the Manufacture of Paper from Wood in the United States, by HENRY T. BROWN, of the "American Artisan." Illustrated by six plates, containing Drawings of Raw Materials, Machinery, Plans of Paper-Mills, etc. etc. 8vo. $5 00

REGNAULT.—ELEMENTS OF CHEMISTRY.

By M. V. REGNAULT. Translated from the French by T. FORREST BENTON, M. D., and edited, with notes, by JAMES C. BOOTH, Melter and Refiner U. S. Mint, and WM. L. FABER, Metallurgist and Mining Engineer. Illustrated by nearly 700 wood engravings. Comprising nearly 1500 pages. In two vols. 8vo., cloth $10 00

REID.—A PRACTICAL TREATISE ON THE MANUFACTURE OF PORTLAND CEMENT:

By HENRY REID, C. E. To which is added a Translation of M. A. Lipowitz's Work, describing a new method adopted in Germany of Manufacturing that Cement. By W. F. REID. Illustrated by plates and wood engravings. 8vo. $7 00

RIFFAULT, VERGNAUD, AND TOUSSAINT.—A PRACTICAL TREATISE ON THE MANUFACTURE OF COLORS FOR PAINTING:

Containing the best Formulæ and the Processes the Newest and in most General Use. By MM. RIFFAULT, VERGNAUD, and TOUSSAINT. Revised and Edited by M. F. MALEPEYRE and Dr. EMIL WINCKLER. Illustrated by Engravings. In one vol. 8vo. (*In preparation.*)

RIFFAULT, VERGNAUD, AND TOUSSAINT.—A PRACTICAL TREATISE ON THE MANUFACTURE OF VARNISHES:

By MM. Riffault, Vergnaud, and Toussaint. Revised and Edited by M. F. Malepeyre and Dr. Emil Winckler. Illustrated. In one vol. 8vo. (*In preparation.*)

SHUNK.—A PRACTICAL TREATISE ON RAILWAY CURVES AND LOCATION, FOR YOUNG ENGINEERS.

By Wm. F. Shunk, Civil Engineer. 12mo., tucks . . $2 00

SMEATON.—BUILDER'S POCKET COMPANION:

Containing the Elements of Building, Surveying, and Architecture; with Practical Rules and Instructions connected with the subject. By A. C. Smeaton, Civil Engineer, etc. In one volume, 12mo. $1 50

SMITH.—THE DYER'S INSTRUCTOR:

Comprising Practical Instructions in the Art of Dyeing Silk, Cotton, Wool, and Worsted, and Woollen Goods: containing nearly 800 Receipts. To which is added a Treatise on the Art of Padding; and the Printing of Silk Warps, Skeins, and Handkerchiefs, and the various Mordants and Colors for the different styles of such work. By David Smith, Pattern Dyer, 12mo., cloth $3 00

SMITH.—THE PRACTICAL DYER'S GUIDE:

Comprising Practical Instructions in the Dyeing of Shot Cobourgs, Silk Striped Orleans, Colored Orleans from Black Warps, ditto from White Warps, Colored Cobourgs from White Warps, Merinos, Yarns, Woollen Cloths, etc. Containing nearly 300 Receipts, to most of which a Dyed Pattern is annexed. Also, a Treatise on the Art of Padding. By David Smith. In one vol. 8vo. $25 00

SHAW.—CIVIL ARCHITECTURE:

Being a Complete Theoretical and Practical System of Building, containing the Fundamental Principles of the Art. By Edward Shaw, Architect. To which is added a Treatise on Gothic Architecture, &c. By Thomas W. Silloway and George M. Harding, Architects. The whole illustrated by 102 quarto plates finely engraved on copper. Eleventh Edition. 4to. Cloth. $10 00

SLOAN.—AMERICAN HOUSES:

A variety of Original Designs for Rural Buildings. Illustrated by 26 colored Engravings, with Descriptive References. By Samuel Sloan, Architect, author of the "Model Architect," etc. etc. 8vo. $2 50

SCHINZ.—RESEARCHES ON THE ACTION OF THE BLAST-FURNACE.

By Chas. Schinz. Seven plates. 12mo. . . . $4 25

SMITH.—PARKS AND PLEASURE GROUNDS:

Or, Practical Notes on Country Residences, Villas, Public Parks, and Gardens. By CHARLES H. J. SMITH, Landscape Gardener and Garden Architect, etc. etc. 12mo. $2 25

STOKES.—CABINET-MAKER'S AND UPHOLSTERER'S COMPANION:

Comprising the Rudiments and Principles of Cabinet-making and Upholstery, with Familiar Instructions, Illustrated by Examples for attaining a Proficiency in the Art of Drawing, as applicable to Cabinet-work; The Processes of Veneering, Inlaying, and Buhl-work; the Art of Dyeing and Staining Wood, Bone, Tortoise Shell, etc. Directions for Lackering, Japanning, and Varnishing; to make French Polish; to prepare the Best Glues, Cements, and Compositions, and a number of Receipts, particularly for workmen generally. By J. STOKES. In one vol. 12mo. With illustrations $1 25

STRENGTH AND OTHER PROPERTIES OF METALS.

Reports of Experiments on the Strength and other Properties of Metals for Cannon. With a Description of the Machines for Testing Metals, and of the Classification of Cannon in service. By Officers of the Ordnance Department U. S. Army. By authority of the Secretary of War. Illustrated by 25 large steel plates. In 1 vol. quarto $10 00

SULLIVAN.—PROTECTION TO NATIVE INDUSTRY.

By Sir EDWARD SULLIVAN, Baronet. (1870.) 8vo. . $1 50

TABLES SHOWING THE WEIGHT OF ROUND, SQUARE, AND FLAT BAR IRON, STEEL, ETC.

By Measurement. Cloth 63

TAYLOR.—STATISTICS OF COAL:

Including Mineral Bituminous Substances employed in Arts and Manufactures; with their Geographical, Geological, and Commercial Distribution and amount of Production and Consumption on the American Continent. With Incidental Statistics of the Iron Manufacture. By R. C. TAYLOR. Second edition, revised by S. S. HALDEMAN. Illustrated by five Maps and many wood engravings. 8vo., cloth $6 00

TEMPLETON.—THE PRACTICAL EXAMINATOR ON STEAM AND THE STEAM-ENGINE:

With Instructive References relative thereto, for the Use of Engineers, Students, and others. By WM. TEMPLETON, Engineer 12mo. $1 25

THOMAS.—THE MODERN PRACTICE OF PHOTOGRAPHY.
By R. W. THOMAS, F. C. S. 8vo., cloth 75

THOMSON.—FREIGHT CHARGES CALCULATOR.
By ANDREW THOMSON, Freight Agent $1 25

TURNING: SPECIMENS OF FANCY TURNING EXECUTED ON THE HAND OR FOOT LATHE:
With Geometric, Oval, and Eccentric Chucks, and Elliptical Cutting Frame. By an Amateur. Illustrated by 30 exquisite Photographs. 4to. $3 00

TURNER'S (THE) COMPANION:
Containing Instructions in Concentric, Elliptic, and Eccentric Turning; also various Plates of Chucks, Tools, and Instruments; and Directions for using the Eccentric Cutter, Drill, Vertical Cutter, and Circular Rest; with Patterns and Instructions for working them. A new edition in 1 vol. 12mo. $1 50

URBIN—BRULL.—A PRACTICAL GUIDE FOR PUDDLING IRON AND STEEL.
By ED. URBIN, Engineer of Arts and Manufactures. A Prize Essay read before the Association of Engineers, Graduate of the School of Mines, of Liege, Belgium, at the Meeting of 1865–6. To which is added a COMPARISON OF THE RESISTING PROPERTIES OF IRON AND STEEL. By A. BRULL. Translated from the French by A. A. FESQUET, Chemist and Engineer. In one volume, 8vo. $1 00

VOGDES.—THE ARCHITECT'S AND BUILDER'S POCKET COMPANION AND PRICE BOOK.
By F. W. VOGDES, Architect. Illustrated. Full bound in pocket-book form. $2 00
In book form, 18mo., muslin 1 50

WARN.—THE SHEET METAL WORKER'S INSTRUCTOR, FOR ZINC, SHEET-IRON, COPPER AND TIN PLATE WORKERS, &c.
By REUBEN HENRY WARN, Practical Tin Plate Worker. Illustrated by 32 plates and 37 wood engravings. 8vo. . . . $3 00

WATSON.—A MANUAL OF THE HAND-LATHE.
By EGBERT P. WATSON, Late of the "Scientific American," Author of "Modern Practice of American Machinists and Engineers," In one volume, 12mo. $1 50

WATSON.—THE MODERN PRACTICE OF AMERICAN MACHINISTS AND ENGINEERS:

Including the Construction, Application, and Use of Drills, Lathe Tools, Cutters for Boring Cylinders, and Hollow Work Generally, with the most Economical Speed of the same, the Results verified by Actual Practice at the Lathe, the Vice, and on the Floor. Together with Workshop management, Economy of Manufacture, the Steam-Engine, Boilers, Gears, Belting, etc. etc. By EGBERT P. WATSON, late of the "Scientific American." Illustrated by eighty-six engravings. 12mo. $2 50

WATSON.—THE THEORY AND PRACTICE OF THE ART OF WEAVING BY HAND AND POWER:

With Calculations and Tables for the use of those connected with the Trade. By JOHN WATSON, Manufacturer and Practical Machine Maker. Illustrated by large drawings of the best Power-Looms. 8vo. $10 00

WEATHERLY.—TREATISE ON THE ART OF BOILING SUGAR, CRYSTALLIZING, LOZENGE-MAKING, COMFITS, GUM GOODS,

And other processes for Confectionery, &c. In which are explained, in an easy and familiar manner, the various Methods of Manufacturing every description of Raw and Refined Sugar Goods, as sold by Confectioners and others $2 00

WILL.—TABLES FOR QUALITATIVE CHEMICAL ANALYSIS.
By Prof. HEINRICH WILL, of Giessen, Germany. Seventh edition. Translated by CHARLES F. HIMES, Ph. D., Professor of Natural Science, Dickinson College, Carlisle, Pa. . . . $1 25

WILLIAMS.—ON HEAT AND STEAM:

Embracing New Views of Vaporization, Condensation, and Expansion. By CHARLES WYE WILLIAMS, A. I. C. E. Illustrated. 8vo. $3 50

WORSSAM.—ON MECHANICAL SAWS:

From the Transactions of the Society of Engineers, 1867. By S. W. WORSSAM, Jr. Illustrated by 18 large folding plates. 8vo. $5 00

WÖHLER.—A HAND-BOOK OF MINERAL ANALYSIS.
By F. WÖHLER. Edited by H. B. NASON, Professor of Chemistry, Rensselaer Institute, Troy, N. Y. With numerous Illustrations. 12mo. $3 00

www.ingramcontent.com/pod-product-compliance
Lightning Source LLC
LaVergne TN
LVHW021412110826
845150LV00007B/1896

* 9 7 8 1 4 2 5 5 1 0 7 7 0 *